Penguin Education X
Penguin Science of

General Editor: B. M. Fo

Clinical Psychology
Editor: Graham A. Foulds

Pathology of Attention

Andrew McGhie

Penguin Science of Behaviour
General Editor: B. M. Foss
Professor of Psychology, Bedford College,
University of London

Abnormal Psychology
Editor: Max Hamilton
Nuffield Professor of Psychiatry,
University of Leeds

Attention and Set
Editor: Anne Treisman
Institute of Experimental
Psychology, University of
Oxford

Clinical Psychology
Editor: Graham A. Foulds
University of Edinburgh

Developmental Psychology
Editor: B. M. Foss
Professor of Psychology,
Bedford College,
University of London

Method and History
Editor: W. M. O'Neil
Deputy Vice-Chancellor,
University of Sydney

Motivation and Emotion
Editors: Dalbir Bindra
Professor of Psychology,
McGill University, Montreal
Jane Stewart
Associate Professor of
Psychology, Sir George
Williams University, Montreal

Perception and Thinking
Editor: P. C. Dodwell
Professor of Psychology,
Queen's University at
Kingston, Ontario

Physiological Psychology
Editor: K. H. Pribram
Research Professor of
Psychology and Psychiatry,
Stanford University

Skills and Learning
Editors: Harry Kay
Professor of Psychology,
University of Sheffield
L. J. Postman
Professor of Psychology,
Institute of Human Learning,
University of California,
Berkeley

Social Psychology
Editor: Michael Argyle
Institute of Experimental
Psychology, University of
Oxford

Pathology of Attention

Andrew McGhie

Penguin Books
Baltimore · Maryland

Penguin Books Ltd, Harmondsworth,
Middlesex, England
Penguin Books Inc., 7110 Ambassador Road,
Baltimore, Md 21207, U.S.A.
Penguin Books Australia Ltd, Ringwood,
Victoria, Australia

First published 1969

Made and printed in Great Britain by
Hazell Watson & Viney Ltd,
Aylesbury, Bucks
Set in Linotype Plantin

Penguin Science of Behaviour

This book is one of the first in an ambitious project, the *Penguin Science of Behaviour,* which will cover a very wide range of psychological inquiry. Many of the short 'unit' texts will be on central teaching topics, while others will deal with present theoretical and empirical work which the Editors consider to be important new contributions to psychology. We have kept in mind both the teaching divisions of psychology and also the needs of psychologists at work. For readers working with children, for example, some of the units in the field of Developmental Psychology will deal with psychological techniques in testing children, other units will deal with work on cognitive growth. For academic psychologists, there will be units in well-established areas such as Learning and Perception, but also units which do not fall neatly under any one heading, or which are thought of as 'applied', but which nevertheless are highly relevant to psychology as a whole.

The project is published in short units for two main reasons. Firstly, a large range of short texts at inexpensive prices gives the teacher a flexibility in planning his course and recommending texts for it. Secondly, the pace at which important new work is published requires the project to be adaptable. Our plan allows a unit to be revised or a fresh unit to be added with maximum speed and minimal cost to the reader.

Above all, for students, the different viewpoints of many authors, sometimes overlapping, sometimes in contradiction, and the range of topics Editors have selected will reveal the complexity and diversity which exist beyond the necessarily conventional headings of an introductory course.

B.M.F.

Contents

Editorial Foreword

Clinical psychology looks both to psychiatrists and to experimental and other psychologists working with normal subjects for help. In his conclusion to this book the author expresses the hope that this debt may soon be repaid. 'In recent years clinical psychology has gained enormously from the expertise and basic methodology of the experimental investigator in the normal field. Perhaps this debt may soon be repaid as the significance of clinical studies for normal mental processes becomes increasingly apparent.' Professor McGhie clearly has in mind his own debt to Broadbent's 'filter' mechanism model of attention on which he and other investigators of attentional defects in schizophrenia have drawn. The contribution of this work to psychiatry is undoubted. Nevertheless, as Professor McGhie points out, 'the clinician is particularly interested in *internal* events and the manner in which the patient samples, orders and interprets his flow of inner stimulation. The effects of emotional and motivational changes of attention are also of great relevance to psychiatric disorder although this is still a relatively unexplored field.' The effective and paranoid disorders are eminently suitable for this work. One of the useful functions of a book such as this – with its systematic coverage of a particular process in different conditions – is to expose these bare patches.

Apart from certain organic psychoses, the most serious of the disorders of attention are found among the schizophrenias. In unimpaired individuals many skills are exercised without recourse to conscious attention. This organizational economy is evidently denied to schizophrenics. They seem to be like a person listening for the first time to a foreign language. The stream of language appears to be very fast and one cannot hear where one word ends and another begins. One tries to attend to small units of speech rather than to grasp the general sense. This problem of redundancy has also engaged experimental clinical psychologists.

A wide range of studies is collated, carefully reviewed and evaluated by the author. His writing, direct and uncluttered by jargon, will, one hopes, contribute to the understanding of normal processes and help in the process of cross-fertilization within psychology.

G.A.F.

Acknowledgements

In preparing a review of this type, one is completely indebted to the industry and wisdom of the many research workers whose work makes such a volume possible. I am also indebted to some of these workers and to their publishers for permission to use their diagrams and tables to illustrate this text. May I also take this opportunity to thank my colleagues for their advice and encouragement, particularly Mr Gordon Lowe whose reading of the text has greatly enhanced its clarity.

Finally, my special thanks to my wife and to my secretary, Miss Irene Henry, who have perhaps suffered most during the preparation of this book.

For the sane man can attend to one thing at a time, can transfer his attention from one thing to another, and compare the two things with one another. It is not always easy to determine in the case of the insane man, whether his sensation or attention be impaired; but the effect remarked, and which may arise from either impairment, ... produces the insanity in such cases.

John Conolly, M.D., in *An Inquiry Concerning the Indications of Insanity*, first published in 1830

Introduction

The role of the clinical psychologist has changed considerably over the last ten years. The earlier clinical psychologists functioned mainly as psychometricians who employed standard psychological tests in their assessments of individual psychiatric patients. This period saw the rapid development of a variety of tests designed to measure the effects of psychiatric illness on selected areas of the patient's personality and mental output. Although these standard tests continue to play an important part in patient assessment, it has become increasingly apparent that the information which they yield is too self-limiting and restricted in its clinical significance. Thus, for example, the I.Q. may act as a useful representation of a patient's current intellectual level. However, this measure of the patient's performance may be influenced by defects in such areas as attention, perception, memory, psychomotor ability, thinking and motivation caused by his present mental condition. Some indications of the specific disorders underlying a low level of intellectual performance may be obtained by a comparison of sub-test scores, but even this will provide only very tentative answers to our question. The psychometric approach is further limited by a problem which is peculiar to test construction in the clinical field. All tests used in the clinical field require to be standardized on both psychiatric and normal control populations. Their efficiency is thus initially dependent upon the accuracy of the criteria used in delineating the diagnostic groups constituting the population in question. Unfortunately the reliability of psychiatric diagnosis is not always high enough to qualify as a stable criterion in test standardization. If clinicians themselves are divided on, let us say, the diagnosis of organic dementia, a psychological test of dementia standardized on clinical judgements of dementia will be unlikely to yield unequivocal findings.

The inadequacies of the present system of psychiatric classification are evident only in some disorders, the reliability of other diagnostic categories being reasonably high. One of the main problems in accurately classifying psychiatric disorders is that the symptoms characterizing some of these disorders are difficult to define and accurately assess. Thus, for example, the term 'dementia' may be used to cover a wide variety of behavioural changes including a decline in intellectual judgement, poor memory, a deterioration in social behaviour and many other changes. 'Retardation', a symptom frequently associated with depressive illnesses, may refer to a slowing down in motor response, in decision making, in the expression of thoughts in speech, in emotional responsiveness and so on. One of the most important tasks facing psychiatry is to develop means of defining and reliably measuring the basic changes in mental processes consequent on mental illness. If psychological research is able to yield reasonably objective means of exploring and objectively assessing the changes in mental functioning demonstrated by patients, it will have made a useful contribution in this direction.

This series on clinical psychology presents the reader with a picture of the present-day level of our knowledge. This present book focuses on pathological changes in attention although it inevitably touches upon other behavioural changes associated with attentive behaviour. The first chapter contains a brief summary of some of the models developed from studies of normal attentive behaviour to provide a background to subsequent discussion.

1 Psychological Models of Attention

Although the concept of attention has engaged the minds of philosophers and psychologists for many years, it is only over the last twenty-five years that psychologists have attempted to investigate systematically attentive behaviour. As long as attention was regarded as a state of narrowed consciousness accessible only to introspection, its components could be subjectively described but not objectively assessed. Nevertheless, introspective analysis of the process of attending produced many ideas which are still being utilized in contemporary research on attention. The phenomenon of habituation by which the brain ceases to register repeated stimuli, the properties which give some stimuli attentive priority over others, and the control of attention by current mood and past experience were discussed by such philosophers as Descartes, Leibnitz and Herbert. Early psychologists such as William James, Ribot and others emphasized the active selective nature of attention and even anticipated much contemporary neuropsychological work by referring to the possibility of taking muscular and postural changes as indirect measures of attention. However, as psychology struggled to attain the respectability of a science, its increasing empiricism and experimental orientation left little room for a process seemingly so dependent upon vagaries of introspection, and attention was relegated to the shadows of the behaviourist's laboratory. In more recent years psychologists have become increasingly concerned with human communication processes and with man's capacity for processing the flow of information reaching him from his environment. In the search for psychological models of man's information-handling potential it soon became obvious that room must be found for a more precise operational concept of the initial attentive process. Theories of attention were subsequently advanced from a variety of different viewpoints by psychologists such as Berlyne (1960), Deutsch and Deutsch (1963) and Broadbent (1958). It is perhaps the latter 'filter' model of attention developed by Broadbent which has presented the most economical and fruitful illustration of the human attentive process. Earlier experimental studies (Hick, 1952; Hyman, 1953; Davis, 1956) had established that the human organism's capacity for handling information and making decisions between alternatives was limited. To function effectively and prevent overloading of our limited processing capacity we are forced to choose from among a variety of competing stimuli reaching the receptors. Using an analogy from mechanical communication systems, Broadbent (1958) called the process of selective attention a *filter* mechanism to underline its function of selecting out the relevant from a number of competing sensory messages. The selected information is fed into the limited capacity decision channel which is connected in turn to a long-term memory store to allow the new information to be integrated with previously stored information (see Figure 1). A great deal of recent psychological research has been concentrated on defining more precisely the manner of operation of this filtering mechanism of attention. A number of experiments have clearly

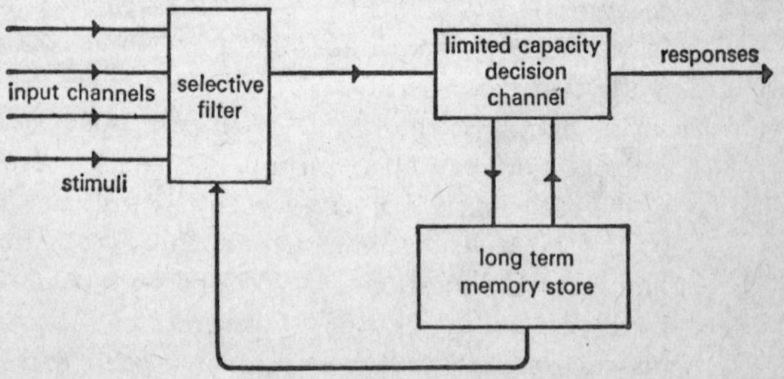

Figure 1 Broadbent's 'filter' and 'information flow' model for selective attention (Broadbent, 1958)

demonstrated that the first stage of attending to two or more competing messages consists of separating the input into discrete channels according to the physical characteristics of the different messages. Thus messages may be distinguished and selectively attended to on the basis of the receptor at which they arrive, their spatial position, their frequency or intensity. Later work suggested that the filtering mechanism of attention further eased the load on the limited capacity decision mechanism by giving priority to stimuli which contain most information at the expense of other signals which, although relevant, are predictable and therefore of low information value. To paraphrase Broadbent, the filter has a permanent bias towards passing novel stimuli. This more complex stage of the filtering operation ensures that attention will be concentrated upon the most relevant or important aspects of any stimulus display. This is particularly important in processing speech when a proportion of most verbal messages are redundant – some words may be easily predicted by their context.

Experimental work (Broadbent and Heron, 1962) has made it clear that the limitation of this part of the human communication channel is an informational one, in that the number of stimuli we can respond to at any one time is determined by the amount of information which these stimuli contain. In other words, it is possible to deal with more than one set of data at a time only if the informational demands of each task are small. Activities which are repeated over a long period of time tend to become automatic and function spontaneously with the minimum utilization of conscious attention. In his analysis of skilled performance, Welford (1958) suggests that the 'decision mechanism of conscious attention is concerned with the resolution of uncertainty.' He describes this process as follows:

More generally the view seems to be tenable that what we recognize as consciousness in the full sense as opposed to merely not being asleep, arises essentially when some uncertainty requires to be resolved, and that the apparent loss of conscious control in highly practical skills is a result of the virtual elimination of uncertainty in performance. On this view, when a performance is so thoroughly learned that it becames 'automatic', it can be carried on while leaving the decision mechanism virtually free.

Thus by repetition and the resolution of uncertainty, conscious attention becomes less bound to concrete stimulation and freer to participate in activities where uncertainty plays a dominant role. Broadbent (1958) has carefully examined the effect of practice on different tasks and agrees that, where practice has removed all uncertainty, no information requires to be processed and the decision mechanism may be short-circuited. Where the activity involved takes the form of a complex but frequently repeated series of actions, Broadbent suggests that the first event in the sequence contains as much information as the entire sequence so that an adequate response can take place without further input. In the language of information theory the later events in the sequence become redundant and do not require either attention or decision making. This is an extremely economical aspect of attention in that quite complex activities may be carried out while the decision mechanism is left free to deal with other more uncertain activities.

Attentional behaviour does not always take the form of selecting a particular class of stimuli from an environment which contains many stimuli competing for attention. Some situations call for sustained attention to one signal in an environment so devoid of distraction as to be monotonous. Prolonged concentration in this type of setting has been studied extensively by experimental psychologists under the general heading of *vigilance*. Such studies were stimulated by the war-time problem of continuous radar scanning and subsequently by the extension of similar signal-detecting tasks in modern industry. As clinicians have commonly reported impairments of sustained attention to be a feature of some groups of psychiatric patients, the findings of such studies are of some interest to clinical psychologists. Studies of tasks requiring vigilance demonstrate that performance tends to decline with time so that the proportion of undetected signals progressively increases. Various theories have been put forward to explain such failures in sustained attention. Broadbent (1958) originally viewed such lapses as an example of the filter's bias towards novel stimuli, the tendency for attention to be attracted by irrelevant distracting stimuli increasing with the time spent on the monotonous vigilance task. More recent studies (Broadbent and Gregory, 1963), based on modern decision theory (Tanner and Swets, 1954), suggest that poor vigilance performance may be due to fluctuations in the subject's level of confidence in his own decisions.

Another aspect of attention which has figured prominently in modern psychological theory is that of *activation* or *arousal* level. Arousal theory proposes that the state of alertness of the individual varies along a continuum from sleep to diffuse excitement. Arousal level is seen to be an important factor in determining the individual's efficiency of performance, this relationship being represented by an inverted U-shaped curve. At low levels of arousal the individual is likely to be inattentive and easily distracted. Very high levels of arousal involve a state of excessive tension and anxiety and performance consequently suffers. At a moderate state of arousal the individual is alert, highly attentive and functioning at an optimal level of efficiency.

Although arousal theory was initiated as a psychological concept its subsequent development has been closely related to modern neurophysiological work on the brain stem reticular activating system (Samuels, 1959). Reviewing the relationship between the reticular system with the process of attention Lord Brain (1958) commented

. . . it looks rather as though its (the reticular system) function were to prepare not only the cortex but the other sensory pathways also to respond to a sensory impulse when it has arrived. As we have seen such responses are at least twofold, namely the reduction of other sensory information which might compete for attention and the integration of the sensory information being attended to with the continuously changing background of somatic and environmental sensory data.

Penfield (1954a) in his concept of the centrencephalic system (embracing the reticular system and its cortical connexions) put forward the hypothesis that

> sensory information is integrated within the centrencephalic system. A selected portion of this information is then somehow projected upwards to the temporal cortex by the portion of the system which is in functional connexion with the temporal cortex of both sides. As it is thus projected, a comparison is made with past similar experiences, thanks to records of the past which are held there, and judgement with regard to familiarity and significance is made.

Subsequent neurophysiological work has made it clear that the reticular system's relationship with the cortex and with the maintenance of consciousness is extremely complex. The examination of the component parts of the reticular system suggests that these may vary in their specialization of function. For example, it now seems likely that the brain stem component performs an alerting operation, while the thalmic sections mediate the focusing and shifting of attention (Lindsley, 1960). Other work (Granit, 1955; Galambos, 1956) has demonstrated that the reticular system is capable of blocking stimulation along sensory pathways near the receptors. However, the regulatory role of the cortex in input processing is also becoming increasingly more apparent. It is now established (Fulton, 1949; French, Hernández-Peón and Livingston, 1955) that pathways from the cortex to the reticular system allow the cortex to exert both a facilitating and inhibiting influence on the reticular system. Other work supports the suggestion that information reaches the cortex prior to its arrival in the reticular system so that the cortex may analyse input and then inhibit its passage through the reticular system, thus blocking attention.

The central role of the cerebral cortex in modifying attention is also evident in the neuropsychological model which has developed out of the interest of Russian psychologists in factors influencing the direction of attention to new stimuli (orienting response; see Lynn, 1966). This model is best represented by Sokolov's (1960) diagrammatic illustration for the operation of orienting responses (Figure 2).

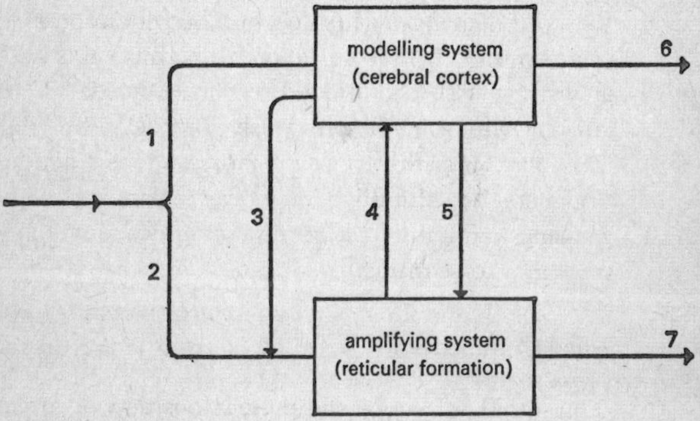

Figure 2 Diagrammatic representation of operation of orienting responses (Sokolov, 1960)

In Sokolov's model, attention is directed by the amplifying mechanism which is assumed to operate in the brain stem reticular formation, the anatomical area known to be crucial for consciousness. However, attention is also seen to be governed by a 'modelling mechanism' in the cerebral cortex which analyses all sensory input and compares it to a permanent neural record of previous input. Incoming stimuli travel along separate pathways to the cerebral cortex (1) and to the reticular formation (2). If the incoming stimulus matches an already existing model (i.e. the stimulus is familiar) the cortex then sends down an inhibiting message (via pathway 3) which blocks the reception of the stimulus at the reticular formation. Where the incoming stimulus does not match with an existing model (i.e. it is novel) the reticular formation is left free to produce the orienting response (via pathway 7). Sokolov does not describe the function of pathway 5 but possibly this pathway might facilitate the orienting response to stimuli which, although matching existing models, have special personal significance for the individual (e.g. Look out!). Pathway 4 represents the ability of the recticular formation to activate the cortex as illustrated by the E.E.G. changes which occur when attention is directed to a stimulus. In Sokolov's model, pathway 6 is designated as dealing with conditioned responses which are made to stimuli which have previously been conditioned. Presumably this pathway would represent the reaction of the organism to stimuli which were part of a habitual sequence and did not require attention for the correct responses to be made.

Final Comments

This rapid review of the present position of attention in modern psychology may give a spurious sense of theoretical order to our rapidly changing view of this initial phase in human information processing. The 'models' of attention which have been discussed here represent some possible interpretations of the limited amount of data gathered to date. Many of the concepts evolved are thinly disguised versions of older ideas, rephrased in the language of modern communication theory. The concept of a 'filter mechanism' has been formulated by other earlier psychologists although in a purely descriptive way. In discussing the operation of consciousness, Freud (1920) referred to the need to accept a cortical mechanism (*Reizschutz*) which, in conjunction with the sense organs, '... operates as a special integument or membrane that keeps off the stimuli, i.e. makes it possible for the energies of the outer world to act with more than a fragment of their intensity on the layers immediately below....' The main benefit of the currently used models of attention is that they are formulated precisely enough to allow their assumptions to be objectively examined. To this extent these theoretical systems have stimulated a great deal of valuable experimentation on the ways in which man samples and selectively responds to the mass of information reaching him from his environment. The emphasis on the processing of *external* information is understandable in so far as a great deal of this work has its roots in practical problems concerned with the monitoring of environmental stimuli. Although the application of this approach to the clinical field has been rewarding, the clinician is particularly interested in *internal* events and the manner in which the patient samples, orders and interprets his flow of inner stimulation. The effects of emotional and motivational changes on attention are also of great relevance to psychiatric disorder athough this is still a relatively unexplored field.

2 The Neuroses and Psychopathy

The Clinical Picture

The broad diagnostic category of neuroses embraces a wide variety of symptoms which cause the patient to experience a general mental and physical state of 'dis-ease'. The symptoms are variable, although anxiety in one form or another is probably the most characteristic feature.

Although a great variety of neurotic syndromes have been discussed in psychiatric literature the three main syndromes are those of anxiety neurosis, hysteria and obsessional neurosis.

Neurotic Syndromes

Anxiety neurosis

As the term implies, the main symptom here is anxiety, which may be 'free-floating' and generalized or 'attached' to specific situations (phobic anxiety). The constant background state of mild anxiety, uneasiness and apprehension may be subject to sporadic exacerbations in the form of panic attacks. The constantly pervasive state of anxiety renders the patient tense, unable to relax, inattentive to environmental change and irritable in his relations with others. The physical components of anxiety reflect autonomic overactivity and include palpitations, respiratory difficulties, headache, and gastric disturbances. Other physical symptoms which may appear under the influence of chronic anxiety are muscular tensions and tremors.

Hysteria

Hysteria may be regarded as a neurotic condition in which the distressing effects of anxiety are avoided by conversion into somatic symptoms. Most hysterical symptoms resemble some organic condition although there is no organic basis for the symptoms. Thus the main symptoms may include paralysis of limbs, loss of hearing or vision, amnesia, fainting and fits, vague unidentifiable somatic pain or the simulation of the symptoms of any organic disease. This type of neurotic condition is frequently termed 'conversion hysteria', both to emphasize its anxiety conversion aspect and to distinguish it from the pattern of traits constituting the 'hysterical personality'. This latter term is used to describe individuals whose personality is distinguished by the presence of traits such as egocentricity, dramatization, emotional lability and over-dependence.

Obsessional neurosis

'Whenever a patient complains of some mental experience which is accompanied by a feeling of subjective compulsion, so that he does not willingly entertain it, but, on the contrary, does his utmost to get rid of it, that is an obsession' (Lewis, 1935). This description of the obsessional neurosis by Aubrey Lewis contains the three cardinal features of the obsessional state – subjective compulsion, attempts to resist the compulsion and retention of insight. Symptoms may take the form of obsessive doubting in which the patient's actions are completely blocked by his inability to decide between alternative courses of action. Alternatively the compulsive element may lead the patient to perform endless meaningless rituals which prevent any other form of productive action.

Psychopathy

Psychopathy is normally designated as a character disorder. It is included with the neuroses here merely because the comparative absence of studies of psychopathic attentional behaviour does not merit its consideration in a separate chapter. As the term *character* disorder implies the primary symptom of psychopathy is an impairment in moral conduct. The term 'symptom' fits uneasily into this context for these patients designated as psychopathic do not feel badly or seek help from society. It is rather that they act badly, causing society to act to protect itself from their psychopathic behaviour. The psychopath's anti-social behaviour is different from that of the delinquent and criminal in that he displays both a lack of feeling towards others and a discouraging inability to learn from experience. His whole personality structure is distinguished by an absence of socialization so that his most noticeable personality traits are egocentricity, inability to control gratification, absence of guilt, and lack of empathy.

Psychological Theories of Neuroses and Psychopathy

Although the psychoanalytic theory of neurotic aetiology has been subject to much criticism, most clinicians still find some modification of the psychodynamic model the most useful in understanding and treating personality disorders. However, in this section we shall consider two alternative explanations of such disturbed behaviour which have more direct relevance to attentional dysfunction.

In 1955 Eysenck put forward a model which attempted to explain personality disorders in terms of conditioned learning theory. Eysenck's system has since been several times modified and elaborated and is now so familiar that a brief summary will serve our present purposes. The concept of cortical inhibition, which played a prominent role in both Pavlovian and Hullian learning theories was further developed by Eysenck to account for individual differences in conditionability. Variations in the build up of inhibitory nervous processes were seen to be associated with differences in personality types, introverts having a slow rate of cortical inhibition and extroverts a rapid rate of inhibition. The slow development and rapid dissipation of inhibition in introverts means that such individuals will tend to condition quickly and easily. In contrast, the extrovert's rapid build up and slow dissipation of inhibition will delay the formation of conditioned habits. On the basis of both theoretical and practical evidence Eysenck has further argued that neurotic introverts tend to develop dysthymic disorders (mainly anxiety and obsessional states) and that neurotic extroverts develop hysterical or psychopathic states. As Eysenck equates neuroticism with autonomic reactivity it can be seen that in the Eysenck model of neurosis, the autonomic nervous system provides the power, and variations in cortical inhibition, the direction. The easily conditioned introvert becomes a conformist whose personality is inhibited and restricted by society while the slow to condition extrovert remains uninhibited and impulsive. The effect of a highly labile autonomic nervous system on the introvert causes him to over-react to all stimuli, particularly to anxiety-provoking stimuli, so that he easily develops conditioned fear responses. Under the same conditions the extrovert will also over-react to stress, but his low conditionability will prevent the establishment of conditioned fear responses. Eysenck's model has stimulated a vast amount of experimental work, the results of which have not always fully supported the original postulates.

Anxiety is the basic symptom in all forms of neuroses, although its form may vary from one type of neurotic condition to another. The development of arousal theory has led to much deliberation regarding the relationship between anxiety and arousal level. Malmo (1957) has suggested that all neurotic conditions in which anxiety is a primary component should be regarded as over-arousal states. Like Eysenck, Malmo utilizes the concepts of central inhibitory mechanisms which he sees as being transmitted by chemical changes in certain cells in the nervous system. Normally the raising of arousal level in the presence of an anxiety-arousing stimulus is followed by the self-correcting action of the inhibitory mechanisms returning arousal to its basal level. If an individual is continually exposed to over-arousing, anxiety-producing stimuli the inhibitory mechanisms, Malmo suggests, will weaken and fail to exert their homeostatic function. This process leads to a chronic anxiety state characterized by an abnormally low threshold for arousal. Thus, the chronically anxious patient will be repeatedly over-aroused by stimuli which would provoke little or no reaction in normal individuals.

It can be seen that Malmo's conception of neurotic anxiety as over-arousal has much in common with Eysenck's theory of the formation of dysthymic symptoms. Both rely heavily on the notion of central inhibitory processes and Malmo's view of arousal is somewhat similar to Eysenck's autonomic lability. Recently Claridge (1967) has developed a theory of neuroses which reinterprets Eysenck's theory in the light of current knowledge of arousal. Claridge's theory and its supporting evidence will be considered in the final section of this chapter which examines some studies of attentional behaviour in neurotic patients.

Investigations of Disturbed Attention in Neuroses

There have been very few reported investigations of attentional changes in neurotic and psychopathic groups. The majority of investigators have accepted Eysenck's distinction between the dysthymic and hysteric-psychopathic forms of neuroses and have explored possible variations of attention and arousal within those neurotic dimensions.

Distractibility

Observations of neurotic patients suggest that their poor concentration is due, not to their being easily distracted by extraneous external stimulation (as in the case with schizophrenic patients), but rather to their preoccupation with their own inner problems. Distraction is thus internally rather than externally located. Cameron and Magaret (1949) found that the performance of normal subjects on a sentence completion task was unaffected by impersonal distraction, in the form of recorded case histories. However, where the distracting stimuli took the form of recordings of the subject's own voice relating his response to T.A.T. (Thematic Apperception Test) cards, performance was noticeably affected (Hassol, Magaret and Cameron, 1952). This form of distractibility was reported to be particularly evident in subjects whose personality descriptions suggested an extroverted personality (Cameron and Magaret, 1950). Foulds (1951) suggested that the introverted neurotic's preoccupation with his inner problems would cause him to be less vulnerable to external distraction. Indeed, external distracting stimulation might lead to an improvement in performance through attracting the patient's attention away from his own thoughts with their potentially higher distracting value. In contrast extroverted neurotics would be more vulnerable to external distraction. Foulds found that dysthymic patients were much slower than hysterics on a modified version of the Porteus Maze Test. However, when subjects were externally distracted by being asked to count aloud while performing the test, the dysthymic patients improved their Maze performance while the hysterics became slower. This is an experimental demonstration of the common clinical observation that anxious patients improve in situations demanding their total involvement.

Vigilance

Surprisingly few studies of vigilance performance of neurotic patients have been reported although the examination of personality variables in normal vigilance suggests that introverts perform better than extroverts. Claridge (1960; Claridge and Herrington, 1963a) has reported two studies of auditory vigilance using neurotic subjects grouped into dysthymic and hysteroid categories. The task used consisted of a thirty-minute recording of random digits presented at a rate of one digit per second.

The target signals to be detected were runs of three consecutive odd digits. Claridge found that the dysthymic patients were significantly superior to normal subjects in their vigilance performance, while the hysterics showed an inferior performance, distinguished by a very rapid falling off in signal detection (group trends illustrated in Figure 3 below). Using measures of skin conductance and heart rate made during vigilance performances, Claridge was also able to show that dysthymics showed a higher level of sympathetic arousal throughout the task.

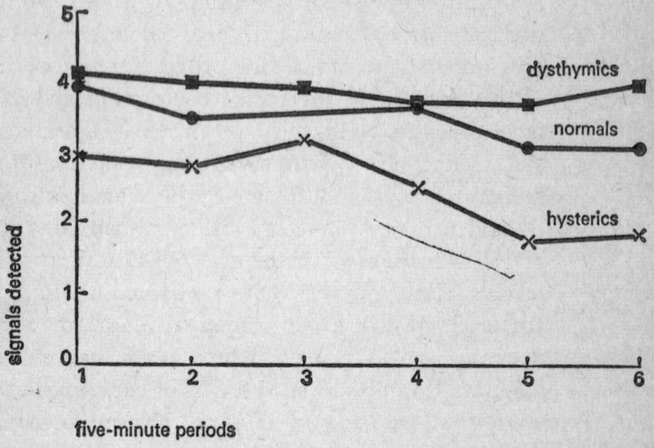

Figure 3 Auditory vigilance curves for dysthymics, hysterics and normal subjects (Claridge, 1967)

Arousal level

Possibly the most ambitious attempt to relate attentional dysfunction to psychiatric symptoms has been put forward by Meldman (1964a, 1964b, 1965) who suggested that all psychiatric disorders should be reclassified as 'diseases of attention'. Neurotic conditions are viewed as conditions of 'selective hyperattentionism', defined as 'the focusing of excessive attention into partial behavioural processes' (Meldman, 1964b). Thus, conversion symptoms represent a focusing of attention on to the affected organ, while obsessional symptoms represent hyperattentionism of certain thoughts. Meldman's terminology is somewhat obscure, but his concept of hyperattentionism appears to be roughly synonymous with increased arousal and heightened anxiety. On the supposition that the organism has available only a fixed amount of 'attentional energy', Meldman explains other neurotic symptoms as a result of 'selective hyperattentionism', an attentional deficit due to the available fund of attentional energy being deployed on one aspect of behaviour. Meldman's only apparent source of support for his attentional theory of neuroses comes from his use of the Necker Cube Test with different groups of psychiatric patients. He suggests (Meldman, 1964a, 1965) that anxiety and phobic states may be differentiated from other neurotic conditions by a high rate of perceptual reversals (more than twenty-eight reversals in a two-minute period) while neurotic depression is represented by an abnormally low reversal rate (less than seventeen reversals in a two-minute period). Detection of the reversing pattern, it is argued, requires a certain amount of attentional energy and therefore the total number of reversals reported gives an indication of the level of hyperattentionism. Other workers have found higher than normal reversal rates in using the Necker Cube Test with neurotic groups (e.g. Eysenck, Granger and Brengelmann, 1957) although some studies have also reported reduced rates (Eysenck, 1947). However, the role of peripheral and central factors in such tests of perceptual oscillation is far from clear and their use in measuring arousal level is very speculative.

Although Melman's attempt to reclassify all psychiatric conditions in terms of attentional changes is highly speculative and over-generalized, his suggestion that neurotics may differ in their arousal level is shared by other more experimentally orientated workers.

Claridge (1967) has suggested that the Eysenckian theory of neuroses might be modified to accommodate recent work on arousal levels. Where Eysenck has emphasized the inhibiting side of the inhibition – excitation balance, Claridge has attempted to examine neurotic groups from the standpoint of differences in the excitatory functions of the nervous system. Noting the correspondence between the concept of cortical excitatory potential (as used by Pavlov, Hull and other learning theorists) and that of arousal, Claridge has carried out a series of investigations of differences in arousal levels within neurotic populations. The reader is referred to Claridge's (1967) recent mongraph giving a full account of his important and interesting studies of arousal variations in different forms of psychiatric illness. Here we will only state briefly some of his findings related to neurotic and psychopathic patients. Two of the techniques used by Claridge to assess arousal level were the sedation threshold and the spiral after-effect. Both these measures have been found to correlate with other measures of arousal level, and the techniques themselves will be examined later (chapter 4, pp. 77 and 79). Claridge's comparisons among normal, dysthymic and hysterico-psychopathic groups on these two measures of arousal are represented in Figures 4 and 5 on page 33.

It can be seen from Claridge's diagrams that dysthymics show a higher sedation threshold and a longer spiral after-effect than normals or hysterics, both these measures indicating a higher level of arousal. Indeed, Claridge found a highly significant positive correlation between the two measures of arousal in his neurotic population. However, this association between the two arousal measures was not apparent in the normal group where the correlation fell to zero. In considering the significance of Claridge's findings it should be kept in mind that his subjects were all male military personnel and therefore a highly selected group not entirely typical of the general neurotic population (a point considered in detail by Claridge himself). Approximately half of his hysterico-psychopathic group have the diagnosis of hysterical personality which some might re-

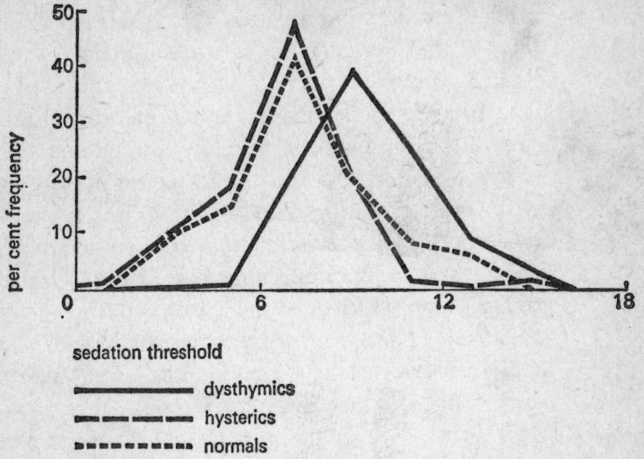

Figure 4 *Frequency distribution for sedation threshold in dysthymics, hysterico-psychopaths and normal subjects (Claridge, 1967)*

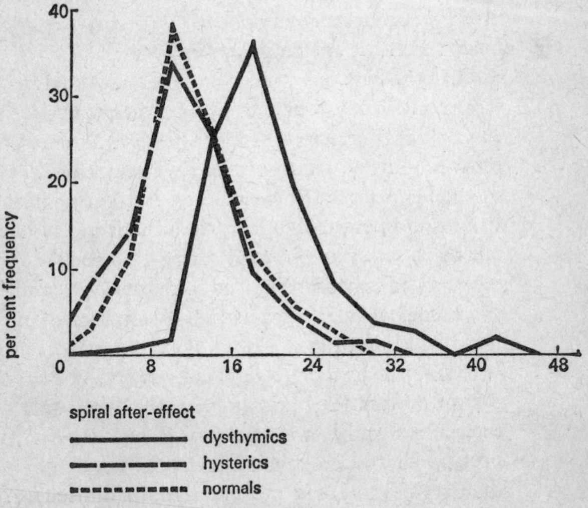

Figure 5 *Frequency distribution for spiral after-effect for dysthymics, hysterics and normal subjects (Claridge, 1967)*

gard as representing a pattern of personality traits rather than a syndrome of psychiatric symptoms. Relatively few (under 5 per cent) of his subjects were diagnosed as psychopathic behaviour disorders, the majority (54 per cent) suffering from anxiety neurosis with some obsessional traits. Sedation threshold and spiral after-effect have both been the target of much criticism as to their reliability as diagnostic instruments. Although Claridge's use of these techniques is aimed at raising the reliability of the measures which they yield, their validity as parameters of arousal is far from being generally acceptable. Nevertheless, Claridge's work has provided a stimulating extension of the original Eysenckian model of neuroses which opens the door to the application of objective research methods to the problem of neurotic illness.

Summary and Conclusions

Compared to other more malignant forms of mental disorder, neurotic and psychopathic conditions have stimulated very little in the way of experimental studies. Most of the investigations which have been reported in this area have been firmly founded in the framework of Eysenck's theory. This paucity of objective research work probably reflects both the highly ambiguous nature of classification in the neuroses and the general view that neurotic symptoms are a result of unconscious dynamic processes not amenable to experimental study. Eysenck's theoretical model, with its emphasis on constitutional and psychophysiological variables, is more conducive to the experimental approach. The only aspect of attentional behaviour to have been studied in a systematic manner is that of arousal level and at the moment the relatively few reported findings are open to several alternative interpretations. Indeed, the cynical observer might conclude that studies of neurotic attention have merely demonstrated that anxious patients are more anxious than non-anxious patients. Although further psychophysiological studies of more clearly defined neurotic symptoms may provide much needed clarification, current offerings appear rather meagre and bland in comparison with the wealth of information on the neuroses accumulated by the more traditional psychodynamic approach.

3 The Affective Psychoses

The Clinical Picture

The affective psychoses represent a group of psychiatric syndromes in which the commonest symptoms consist of changes in the affective or mood state of the patient. The mood changes may range from depressive feelings to the opposite affective pole of elation. In the classical form of *manic-depressive* illness the patient alternates between the two extremes of mania and depression with intervening periods of normality.

However, the classical form of manic-depressive psychosis with its pronounced cyclical changes is not common and probably accounts for a very small proportion of patients who are diagnosed under the affective psychoses. In the majority of cases of affective psychosis the illness takes the form of either depression or more rarely mania, with no cyclical variation between the two mood states. Some patients suffer from a single depressive or manic illness, while in others periodic attacks are evident.

Psychiatrists frequently make a distinction between this form of psychotic (endogenous) depression and a neurotic (reactive) depression which is a more transient reaction to a specific environmental stress. Although psychotic and neurotic depressive illnesses are said to be distinguished by differences in diurnal variation of symptoms, sleep rhythm and family history, the differential diagnosis is in practice often extremely difficult. Indeed, clinicians are still very divided in their agreement as to whether these two types of depression constitute separate disease entities or merely represent end points on a continuum of severity of the depressive symptoms.

Studies of Attentional Changes in the Affective Psychoses

The length of this section reflects the overall negative findings of most studies of attentional dysfunction in the affective psychoses. The depressive patients included as controls in the investigations of distraction in schizophrenia reported by McGhie and his colleagues (see chapter 4, page 59) were found to perform at a normal level on a variety of cognitive tests. Other studies of psychotic patients have also reported depressed patients as being no more distractible than normal subjects (Payne, 1961; Shakow, 1963). Although depressed patients are found to be slower in their performance on most types of tasks, such retardation would appear to be a feature of psychotic patients in general. Indeed Payne (1961) has suggested that Eysenck's 'psychotism' factor can be equated with retardation. These observations accord with those of others such as Friedman (1964) who reports that although those patients complain of inadequacy and constantly criticize their own performance, they will under persuasion perform as well as normals on most tasks. The few investigations of variations in attention in manic patients tend to report (McGhie, Chapman and Lawson, 1964) that, although the manic patient is constantly distracted by his inner mental state he shows little tendency to be abnormally distracted by externally imposed, extraneous stimulation.

There have been relatively few investigations of the arousal level of affective psychotics, although some reports suggest a lowered level of autonomic arousal in psychotic depressive illness. Most of this evidence comes from studies using the sedation threshold technique developed by Shagass (1954). Although some workers have found no difference between the sedation thresholds of psychotic depressives and neurotic and normal samples (Ackner and Pampiglione, 1959) others have reported a lower threshold in psychotic than in neurotic depression (Shagass and

Jones, 1958). Claridge (1967) suggests that neurotic depression might be associated with overactivity of the reticular arousal system and psychotic depression with a low level of arousal.

Summary and Conclusions

There would appear to be no evidence to suggest that attentional dysfunction is a characteristic feature of the affective psychoses, although the clinically observable, poor attentive behaviour of manic patients has not been systematically studied. The possible distinction of neurotic and psychotic depressives in terms of arousal level requires further study with more careful control of the clinical variables said to distinguish these two diagnostic groups.

4 Schizophrenia

The Clinical Picture

Although the first classification of schizophrenia as a separate disease entity was due to the work of Kraepelin (1896), the existence of a form of insanity affecting young people had been increasingly recognized during the latter half of the ninteenth century. One of the earliest descriptions of this condition, characterized by its early onset and progressive dementia, is contained in Rousseau's (1857) thesis. In the next few years various terms were put forward to describe this condition; Morel (1860) called it 'démence précoce', Hecker (1871) used the term 'Hebephrenia' and Kahlbaum (1874) referred to 'katatonia' in describing a similar syndrome characterized by a lesser degree of deterioration. It fell to Kraepelin (1896) to unify these various observations, using Morel's category of 'dementia praecox' to describe a single disease entity containing most of the symptoms previously noted:

> Under the term dementia praecox, we arrange a series of disease pictures, whose common characteristic is a termination in a peculiar weakened state of mind. This unfavourable outcome need not occur in every instance, but is nevertheless so exceedingly frequent as to justify our holding fast to this general name.

However, Bleuler's (1911) detailed clinical studies of dementia praecox patients convinced him of the inadvisability of placing the main emphasis on outcome as a retrospective diagnostic criterion. He therefore attempted to define the main *symptoms* of the illness in order that diagnosis could be based on the current mental state and its earlier precursors. Bleuler's observations led him to define three primary symptoms as being most characteristic of this psychotic condition – thought disorder, flattening or inappropriateness of affect and loss of volition. These he saw as being a consequence of 'a splitting off of the different psychic functions' so that the cognitive, affective and volitional functions ceased to operate in a unitary, congruous way. Other symptoms, such as hallucinations and delusions, were regarded by Bleuler as secondary symptoms, not specific to this type of psychiatric illness. Bleuler was less convinced than Kraepelin of the inevitability of the progressive dementia. Such observations led him to suggest that the term dementia praecox be replaced by the term *schizophrenia* which laid less stress on the terminal state of dementia and highlighted the 'splitting' process which he regarded as the basic characteristic of this illness. Bleuler also developed Kraepelin's sub-division of hebephrenia, catatonia, and paranoid schizophrenia and accepted the inclusion of a fourth subcategory – 'simple schizophrenia'. The hebephrenic subtype included patients whose main symptoms were thought disorder and flattening or inappropriateness of affect. The onset of this form of schizophrenia is early, the course of its development insidious and its prognosis poor. In many ways hebephrenia closely corresponds to Kraepelin's original concept of dementia praecox and is usually regarded as the most malignant form of schizophrenia. The term catatonic schizophrenia characterized those patients whose most noticeable symptom was a disturbance of motor activity, the most frequent form of which was seen in motor blocking, stereotyped posturing or complete stupor. The paranoid category characterized patients whose primary symptom was that of delusional thinking, other disturbances of thinking, feeling or volition being less conspicuous or even totally absent. The sub-category of 'simple' schizophrenia was added to include patients whose behaviour showed impoverishment or shallowness of emotional response and a lack of drive in the absence of more florid symptoms. Bleuler's classification made schizophrenia a much wider diagnostic concept than Kraepelin's dementia praecox, and led to its being applied to a larger, more diversified group of patients.

Bleuler's detailed studies of the cardinal symptom of schizophrenia greatly clarified its classification as a disease entity. The final link in establishing the syndrome as a disease process was provided by Meyer's (1906, 1910) work on the natural history of schizophrenia. Meyer drew attention to the premorbid personality of the schizophrenic patient and illustrated how the final psychosis gradually emerged from an abnormal personality structure. His work led to a fuller consideration of the social adjustment factors which help to make manifest the latent psychotic condition.

In his observations of schizophrenic patients, Bleuler became so impressed with the heterogeneous nature of this diagnostic group that he was careful to refer to 'the group of schizophrenias'. Although a great deal of subsequent work has further undermined the view that schizophrenia can be regarded as an aetiological unity, there has been a continuing tendency to use the term as if it did represent a specific disease entity. The application of the four subcategories might appear to act as a palliative, but the degree of overlap between these sub-categories greatly lowers their diagnostic reliability. Some psychiatrists have argued that patients whose illness is characterized by delusional thinking, in the absence of primary schizophrenic symptoms, should be grouped under the category of 'paranoid psychosis' as distinct from schizophrenia. Proponents of this argument emphasize that the paranoid group tend to have a later onset of their illness (nearer middle-age), rarely show any tendency towards deterioration and tend to be of somewhat higher intelligence than schizophrenic patients. The 'simple' sub-category is particularly dubious and may too easily lead to diagnostic confusion with patients who have a markedly inadequate personality structure. Other clinicians have suggested that catatonia may appear more as a transient symptom during any schizophrenic illness and does not merit inclusion as a distinct diagnostic sub-category.

The lack of cohesive unity of schizophrenia and the unacceptable nature of the traditional sub-categories has led to the advancement of a number of alternative systems of sub-classification. Although some of these attempts have had the healthy effect of stimulating more careful and intensive observations of the behaviour of schizophrenic patients, the systems themselves have tended to be too highly complex and subjective to be of great practical value. Later in this chapter we shall examine some less ambitious, but probably more useful, methods of differentiating within the schizophrenic group.

The outlook for schizophrenic patients today is regarded as a great deal less gloomy than in the late nineteenth and early twentieth century. Modern advances in social care and in the use of drugs have ensured a much more hopeful outlook for many patients. However, the ultimate goal of all research into schizophrenia is still to discover its basic cause and thus to arrive at a rational method of treatment.

Some clinicians, particularly in the U.S.A., have approached schizophrenia from a psychodynamic viewpoint, seeking to find the aetiology of schizophrenia in the patient's early learning experiences. Much attention has been given to the family background of schizophrenic patients and observations of disturbed family dynamics have led to the examination of the 'schizophrenogenic' influences within the family pattern which are taken to produce the schizophrenic breakdown of one member (Bateson, Jackson, Haley and Weakland, 1956). The evidence in favour of a predominantly psychogenic aetiology of schizophrenia has been critically reviewed by Kind (1966).

In contrast to this approach, others have emphasized the organic and constitutional determinants of schizophrenia, seeking evidence of a biological disorder which causes a malfunctioning of the brain and nervous system.

This approach has led to a number of hypotheses suggesting a biochemical pathology in which schizophrenia is seen as the end result of a toxic process produced by a metabolic disorder (Smythies, 1967). A further extension of this approach is seen in the many genetic studies which aim at identifying the mode of transmission of the pathological organic process.

Much valuable work on schizophrenia is unfortunately blurred by the tendency of contributors to wear blinkers which effectively screen out any findings which are not based on their own (organic *or* psychogenic) assumptions. The unnecessary and weak nature of this 'either – or' approach to schizophrenic aetiology has been clearly put by Maher (1966) in discussing genetic studies:

> As long as the question is posed as being whether schizophrenic behaviour is genetically determined *or* environmentally determined there seems to be little prospect that we shall advance much further in our understanding of any of its determinants. We do have ample evidence that manipulations of biological variables produces changes in behaviour; we also have ample evidence that manipulating the environment changes behaviour. The important problem is the discovery of the processes by which these influences operate and the nature of the interaction between them (Maher, 1966).

However, probably the greatest obstacle to all aetiological research in schizophrenia is the non-homogeneous nature of patients included in its confines. Since schizophrenia is a blanket term possibly embracing a number of conditions each with its own aetiology, any approach which ignores this heterogeneity is bound to yield contradictory and confusing findings. The establishment of a reliable system of sub-classifying the schizophrenias would appear to be a necessary precursor to aetiological studies. This position has been stated by Tait (1958) who, in reviewing the physiopathology of schizophrenia wrote:

> I do not personally believe that one single biochemical answer to what we call schizophrenia will be found. The biochemist

and the electrophysiologist are more likely to give us a set of answers, and I could wish we were in a position to give them a set of questions which were equally precise and clearly defined. I feel that we must exploit old or develop new methods of defining and measuring our schizophrenic states (Tait, 1958).

Psychological studies may contribute to this process of delineating schizophrenia by producing reliable measurements of the changes in mental functioning occurring in different forms of the psychosis. The remainder of this chapter presents some of the findings of such investigations into the attentional behaviour of schizophrenic patients.

Observational Studies

A common stereotype of the schizophrenic patient is that he is an individual who lives in a completely self-contained, phantasy world of his own making – 'a dreamer in a world awake' whose attention is withdrawn from external reality and directed inwards. However, this stereotype is flatly contradicted by clinicians who have made intensive studies of schizophrenic patients. Bleuler (1911) described disturbances of attention in schizophrenic patients as follows:

> At the one extreme patients are easily distractible, seem to lack directives of their own and depend entirely on outer impressions; ... at the other extreme they are undistractible and even the strongest stimuli will fail to influence their train of ideas or arouse their attention ... lack of distractibility may appear to spring from the patient's lack of interest: as if they care about nothing, nothing can influence their behaviour. But it can be shown that the same patients understand very well what goes on about them, even when they pay no active attention.

He also noted that 'even although uninterested and autistically encapsulated patients appear to pay little attention to the outside world, they register a remarkable number of events of no concern to them. The selection which attention exercises over normal sensory impressions may be reduced to zero, so that almost everything that meets the senses is registered.' Schilder (1951) described schizophrenic patients as unable to pursue 'the determinative idea' in so far as they were constantly at the mercy of ideas subsidiary to the mainstream of their thinking. In a series of clinical studies of chronic schizophrenic patients Freeman, Cameron and McGhie (1958) described a state of undifferentiated attention which causes the patient to confuse internal mentality and external reality. In a later study by Freeman, Cameron and McGhie (1966) it was suggested that impaired capacity to sustain attention was one of the most distinctive features of schizophrenic patients.

Vivid illustrations of disturbed attentional behaviour were provided by another systematic study, in which young schizophrenic patients described the difficulties they encountered during the early stages of their illness (McGhie and Chapman, 1961).

When these patients were encouraged to describe recent changes in their own experiences their reports referred most frequently to a disturbance in the normal process of selective attention. Although patients described their difficulties in different ways the following extracts are typical:

'I can't concentrate. It's diversion of attention that troubles me . . . the sounds are coming through to me but I feel my mind cannot cope with everything. It is difficult to concentrate on any one sound . . . it's like trying to do two or three different things at the one time.'

'It's as if I'm too wide awake – very, very alert. I can't relax at all. Everything seems to go through me. I just can't shut things out.'

'Everything seems to grip my attention although I am not particularly interested in anything. I'm speaking to you just now but I can hear noises going on next door and in the corridor. I find it difficult to shut these out and it makes it more difficult for me to concentrate on what I am saying to you.

Often the silliest things going on seem to interest me. That's not even true; they won't interest me but I find myself attending to them and wasting a lot of time this way. I know that sounds like laziness but it's not really.'

Many of the patients also described allied perceptual changes, such as a heightening of sensory vividness; involuntary awareness of features in the perceptual field which had hitherto occupied a background position. The following few comments are again illustrative of the general pattern:

'During the last while back I have noticed that noises all seem to be louder to me than they were before. It's as if someone had turned up the volume ... I notice it most in background noises – you know what I mean, noises that are always around you but you don't notice them. Now they seem to be just as loud and sometimes louder than the main noises that are going on ... it's a bit alarming at times because it makes it difficult to keep your mind on something when there's so much going on that you can't help listening to.'

'Have you ever had wax in your ears for a while and then had them syringed? That's what it's like now, as if I had been deaf before. Everything is much noisier and it excites me.'

'The colours of things seem much more clearer and brighter ... maybe it's because I notice so much more about things and find myself looking at them for a long time. Not only the colour of things fascinates me but all sorts of little things, like markings on the surface, pick up my attention too.'

Similar descriptions have been noted by others who have studied the self-reports of schizophrenic patients. Bowers and Freedman (1966) quote the following example: 'My senses were sharpened, I became fascinated by the little insignificant things around me ... sights and sounds possessed a keenness that I had never experienced before ... my senses were sharpened, sounds were more intense and I could see with great clarity, everything seemed very clear to me. Even my sense of taste seemed more acute.'

Another patient, now recovered, described her illness in the following manner: 'What I do want to explain if I can is the exaggerated state of awareness in which I lived before, during, and after my acute illness. It was as if parts of my brain awoke which had been dormant, and I became interested in a wide assortment of people, events, places and ideas which normally would make no impression on me' (McDonald, 1960).

Patients in the McGhie and Chapman study also reported disturbance of their bodily movements and general motility.

'I'm not sure of my own movements any more. It's very hard to describe this but at times I'm not sure about even simple actions like sitting down. It's not so much thinking out what to do it's the doing of it that sticks me . . . I found recently that I was thinking of myself doing things before I would do them. If I'm going to sit down for example, I've got to think of myself and almost see myself sitting down before I do it. It's the same with other things like washing, eating and even dressing – things that I have done at one time without even bothering or thinking about at all . . . I take more time to do things because I am always conscious of what I am doing. If I could just stop noticing what I am doing, I would get things done a lot faster.'

'I have to do everything step by step now, nothing is automatic. Everything has to be considered.'

One patient who had been a keen athlete prior to his illness declared 'when I am racing and am ready to get off the mark I have to think of putting my hands down in front of me and how to lift my legs before I can start. People just do things but I have to watch first to see how they do things. I have to think out most things first and know how to do things before I do them.'

Such descriptions of disturbance in motor behaviour were interpreted by McGhie and Chapman in the following manner:

The loss of spontaneity in behaviour which schizophrenic patients describe, would seem to be a natural consequence of their conscious attention being invaded by the volitional impulses and stimuli from the effectors which normally function autonomously outside the range of awareness. The patient now has consciously to initiate and control his bodily movements, every one of which involves a decision. Activities which before were self-regulative are now experienced as uncertain and requiring deliberate co-ordination. It is small wonder that the patient speaks of a split between his mind and body, and feels that he is in danger of losing control over his own actions.

In terms of Kubie's (1954) psychoanalytic view of the development of skilled acts, these patients may be said to be describing an invasion of conscious awareness by preconscious processes. In his analysis of normal skill, Welford (1958) suggests that the decision mechanism of consciousness is concerned with 'the resolution of uncertainty'. Economy of mental effort is achieved by many actions being so thoroughly learned that their operation becomes automatic and no longer requires conscious intervention. The reports of schizophrenic patients suggest that the former certainty in well-rehearsed skills has broken down; everything is now uncertain and requires conscious attention and decision making.

Thought disorder is perhaps the most distinctive feature of schizophrenia. The comments of some of the patients in the McGhie and Chapman study not only provide vivid descriptions of the form of schizophrenic thought disorder but suggest its association with a primary disorder of attention.

'My thoughts get all jumbled up. I start thinking or talking about something but I never get there. Instead I wander off in the wrong direction and get caught up with all sorts of different things that may be connected with the things I want to say but in a way I can't explain.'

'My trouble is that I've got too many thoughts. You might think about something, let's say that ashtray and just think, oh yes, that's for putting my cigarette in, but I would think of it and then I would think of a dozen different things connected with it at the same time.'

One patient summed up his difficulties in the following telling comment – 'When I'm trying to think of something

I'm like a railway engine, running along a line where someone keeps changing the points.'

Theoretical Interpretation of Observational Studies

In attempting to give a unified interpretation of the different reports of changed mental functioning given by their young schizophrenic patients, McGhie and Chapman postulated on the role of attention in maintaining effective environment contact.

> By the process of attention we thus break down and effectively categorize both the information reaching us from the environment, and that which is internally available in the form of stored past experience. By such processes we reduce, organize and interpret the otherwise chaotic flow of information reaching consciousness to a limited number of differentiated, stable and meaningful percepts from which reality is constructed. Now let us suppose that there is a breakdown in this selective-inhibitory function of attention. Consciousness would be flooded with an undifferentiated mass of incoming sensory data, transmitted from the environment via the sense organs. To this involuntary tide of impressions there would be added the diverse internal images, and their associations, which would no longer be coordinated with incoming information. Perception would revert to the passive and involuntary assimilative process of early childhood and, if the incoming flood were to carry on unchecked, it would gradually sweep away the stable constructs of a former reality.

Similar suggestions of the cardinal role of attention dysfunction in schizophrenic patients have been made by other clinical investigators. Freeman, Cameron and McGhie (1966) summarized their psychoanalytic study of schizophrenic patients as follows:

> Clinical observation suggests that there are ... two forms of disturbance of attention and concentration in mental illness. ... In the first type, which is most usually encountered in psychoneurosis and non-psychotic illnesses, the disturbance of attention is the result of the impact of repressed conflicts. In the second type, the attentional defect is the end result of an

impairment of cognitive functioning.... The (schizophrenic) patient frequently makes it clear that he is a recipient of a flood of stimuli. Registration and perception are no longer separate activities but seem to run into one another.

Later Freeman suggests that one of the most distinctive features of schizophrenic behaviour is that attention 'is reduced to a process of passive assimilation.' He also makes a useful distinction between the behaviour of the schizophrenic and the manic patient who superficially appears to show the same type of attention disturbance:

When the distractibility of the manic or hypomanic patient is scrutinized it becomes apparent that he is constantly scanning the environment for sources of stimulation. It is the rapid movement of attention from one subject to the next that constitutes the distractibility.... In mania and hypomania, attention is not passively attracted to objects but is actively directed to them. This stands in contrast to schizophrenic patients whose attention is passively tied to hallucinating experiences or to falsified perceptions.

Lehmann (1966) suggests that the schizophrenic patient has:

a primary, possibly constitutional, susceptibility ... to be subjected to the impact of a higher number of discrete sensory stimuli per time unit of experience than most other pathological or non-pathological individuals. If he is capable of coping with this greater than average influx of discrete sensory stimuli, he might perform at a better than average level but when the extraordinary sensitivity of his receptive apparatus is not matched by an equally extraordinary performance of his central processing apparatus, then his integration breaks down and he may become psychotic.

McDonald (1960), already quoted above, gives the following lucid and interesting interpretation of her own experiences during the time she was ill:

Each of us is capable of coping with a large number of stimuli, invading our being through any of the senses.... It's obvious that we would be incapable of carrying on any of our daily activities if even one hundredth of all these available stimuli invaded us at once. So the mind must have a filter, which functions without our conscious thought, sorting stimuli and allowing only those which are relevant to the situation in hand to disturb consciousness. What happened to me in Toronto was a breakdown of the filter, and a hodge-podge of unrelated stimuli were distracting me from things that should have held my undivided attention. . . . I had very little ability to sort the relevant from the irrelevant. . . . Completely unrelated events became intricately connected in my mind.

Such observations suggest that schizophrenic patients experience a widening of attention which affects many other areas of their behaviour. However, they also raise many questions, some of which are difficult to answer by direct observations. Are such impairments of attention specific to schizophrenia or do they recur in other psychiatric patients – or for that matter, in normal subjects in certain conditions? Is the schizophrenic disorder of attention unitary or does it vary with other situational factors? For example, does attention fluctuate with the modality in which stimuli are presented? What is the effect of disturbance of selective attention on other mental functions, such as perception, memory, motor performance, language and so on? To what extent is the quality and degree of attentional impairment associated with the severity, the duration or the form of the schizophrenic illness? In order to answer these and other related questions we turn next to studies which have employed the experimental approach.

Experimental Studies

Overinclusive thinking

One of the first experimental workers to suggest that the poor cognitive performance of schizophrenic patients might be due to an underlying impairment in attention was Norman Cameron (1938, 1939). Earlier studies had concluded that schizophrenic thinking was characterized by an impoverishment of concept formation and an inability to think abstractly. On the basis of his own more intensive studies of their performance on various category sorting tasks, Cameron suggested that schizophrenic patients were handicapped by their unwillingness or their inability to confine their conceptual thinking within the narrow range of concepts set by the sorting tests. He was able to demonstrate that the schizophrenic patient's poor performance on such tests was a result of his tendency to formulate concepts which were either based on peripheral and irrelevant features of the objects, or upon personal associations with the objects. Thus the patient might group together such objects as a fountain-pen, a knife and fork and a pipe on the grounds that 'you go to the fountain to drink after you have eaten your dinner and the water has to be piped out.' Faced with the task of grouping wooden blocks according to size, shape or colour he would tend to base his classification on inconsequential details, such as scratches and irregularities on the blocks. Cameron suggested that the schizophrenic patient suffered, not from impoverishment in concept formation, but rather from an over-abundance of loose concepts of his own making. He referred to the schizophrenic patient's 'inability to preserve conceptual boundaries' and put forward the term *overinclusive* to describe this feature of schizophrenic thinking. Cameron also suggested that the patient's behaviour might be explained in terms of a primary disorder of attention, the schizophrenic being unable to focus attention on that part of the environment relevant to the current task. Later a number of attempts were made to devise specific measures of overinclusion. Zaslow (1950) used a series of cards, the first depicting a triangle and the last a circle, with the shapes on the intervening cards gradually changing from a triangle to a circle. Zaslow predicted that if schizophrenic patients were asked to sort the cards into the two categories of triangles and circles, their overinclusive tendencies would lead them to include more cards in each of the two categories. In a comparison between schizophrenic patients and normal subjects this hypothesis was verified. Chapman (1956) and Chapman and Taylor (1957) utilized another form of card sorting test in measuring overinclusion in schizophrenic patients. Subjects were provided with four stimulus cards, each of which had objects printed on the four corners, and a pack of cards again containing a picture on each corner. Instructions were to ignore all the pictures on the stimulus cards except the picture on one corner. The response cards which had to be sorted on to the categories shown by the stimulus cards contained a varying number of items matching irrelevant items on the stimulus cards. As predicted, schizophrenic patients were distracted by the irrelevant items on the response cards.

The most intensive series of studies of overinclusive thinking were carried out by Payne and his colleagues (1960–64). In order to elicit the most characteristic feature of schizophrenic thought disorder Payne and Hewlett (1960) administered a large battery of psychological tests to groups of schizophrenic patients, neurotics, non-schizophrenic psychotic patients and normal controls. Their battery included tests of intelligence, retardation, concrete thinking and overinclusion. A factor analysis of the resultant data showed that only the 'overinclusive' factor successfully discriminated the schizophrenic patients from all other groups. However, an inspection of the individual test scores suggested that only about half of the schizophrenic patients were abnormally overinclusive, the remainder having scores within the normal range. Those schizophrenic patients who were not abnormally overinclusive had high loadings on a second factor of retardation. These findings led Payne and Hewlett to postulate a two-factor theory of schizophrenic thought disorder, some schizophrenic patients being abnormally overinclusive and the remainder being abnormally slow and retarded.

In a later study Payne (1964) investigated the association between overinclusive thinking and the span of attention. Groups of patients were presented with brief tachistoscopic exposures of pictures and invited to identify the picture as early as possible in a series of exposures of increasing length. Payne argued that overinclusive schizophrenics would have a widened span of attention and thus process more information than others on each exposure. Taking the earliest point in the exposure series where the patient attempts to identify the picture as an index of the amount of information being processed, Payne found a very high correlation (+0·90) between this measure of 'perceptual overinclusion' and his standard measures of overinclusive thinking.

In surveying a number of his studies Payne concluded that overinclusive thinking is basically a disturbance not of thinking but of the normal process of selective attention:

> The mechanism of attention itself seems to become defective. Whatever filtering mechanism ensures that only the stimuli (internal or external) that are relevant to the task enter consciousness and are processed, it seems no longer able to exclude the irrelevant. This has numerous repercussions. Thinking becomes distracted by external events. It also becomes distracted by irrelevant personal thoughts and emotions which may even become mixed up with the problem. Selective perception becomes impossible so that instead of dealing with the essence of the problem, irrelevant aspects are perceived and thought about . . . (Payne, 1964).

Perceptual constancy

Further experimental evidence of an attentional deficit in schizophrenia may be derived from a series of studies of perceptual anomalies in psychotic patients. These investigations (Weckowicz, 1957; Weckowicz, Somner and Hall, 1958) demonstrated a reduction in both size and distance constancy in schizophrenic patients as compared with other psychotic patients and normal controls. This finding is in accordance with the reports of schizophrenic patients (McGhie and Chapman, 1961) that their world now seemed flat, lacking depth and that approaching objects appeared to change in size in an alarming manner. Such changes in the perceptual constancy of schizophrenic patients was confirmed and elaborated by other investigators (Crookes, 1957; Hamilton, 1963). Weckowicz and Whitney (1960) have also demonstrated an increase of the illusory effect in the Müller-Lyer illusion with schizophrenic patients. Susceptibility to the illusion was presumed to indicate a reduced ability to ignore the irrelevant lines and to attend selectively to the irrelevant part of the figure. In another study Weckowicz (1960) found schizophrenic patients to do much worse than other psychiatric patients on a task involving the identification of forms embedded in an irrelevant background, although their perception of the figures in the absence of a distracting background was unimpaired.

Weckowicz suggested that these and other findings on perceptual anomalies in schizophrenic patients were related to a common deficit of *perceptual selectivity* and that this failure should also be evident in the thought process where abstract thinking is dependent upon a high degree of selectivity. Some support for this hypothesis was found in an investigation (Weckowicz and Blewett, 1959) into the association between reduced perceptual constancy and impaired concept formation. Here it was found that schizophrenic patients with poor perceptual constancy performed very poorly on tests of conceptual thinking.

Such findings led to the following formulation of an attentional breakdown in schizophrenia:

There is a redundancy of information in the sensory input from the environment to the organism. The 'cognitive process' is to a great extent concerned with the reduction of this redundancy and with 'selection' or 'abstraction' of some information according to certain principles and suppression of all other information. In the perceptual process it will manifest itself in the ability to see stable 'things' or objects in spite of a constant change in the sensory input – the ability which is usually described as 'constancy of perception'.... Their (schizophrenic's) perception is more influenced by the here and now factors of the immediate situation and less by the experience of the past and the anticipation of the future. ... There is some change in the filtering of stimulation. ... The gates are open wide, the cortex is flooded with irrelevant information so that maintenance of set becomes difficult! (Weckowicz and Blewett, 1959).

Distraction studies

Payne and Caird (1967) have recently extended the investigation of overinclusive thinking in examining its association with distractibility. Starting from the Rodnick and Shakow (1940) suggestion that the slow reaction times of schizophrenic patients is due to their being distracted by irrelevant internal and external stimuli, Payne hypothesized that overinclusive schizophrenics would show a progressive slowness in reaction time responses as experimentally imposed distractions are increased. The subjects studied formed a group of acute schizophrenic patients who had been graded for overinclusion on one of Payne and Hewlett's (1960) tests. An auditory reaction-time task was employed to test both simple and complex reaction-time responses. Padded earphones and blindfolds were used to reduce the influence of any chance environmental distractors to a minimum. Alternative types of distraction conditions were used in which the distracting stimulus varied between a meaningless auditory tone of variable intensity and a tape recording of meaningful conversation. Although the effect of distraction on reaction time was found to be more pronounced in schizophrenic patients with high overinclusive scores it did not reach an acceptable level of statistical significance in all the distracting conditions. Furthermore, in the distraction-free condition (blindfold and padded earphones) the overinclusive patients produced slower reaction times. Contrary to Payne and Caird's expectation the non-overinclusive group of schizophrenics were also significantly effected by some of the distracting conditions. The main results of this investigation are illustrated in Figure 6.

A possible explanation, put forward by Payne and

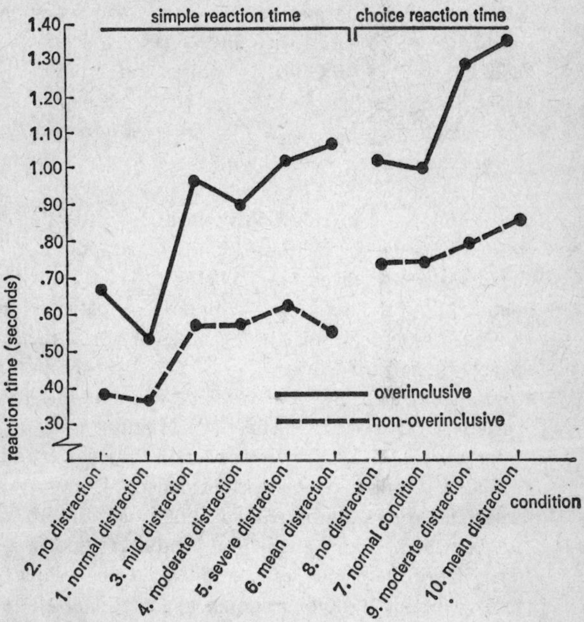

Figure 6 Effects of distraction on reaction time for overinclusive and non-overinclusive schizophrenic patients (Payne and Caird, 1967)

Caird, is that the demarcation of the patients into 'overinclusive' and 'non-overinclusive' on the basis of their overinclusive test scores is too crude and leads to information being lost. Support for this interpretation is contained in Payne and Caird's findings that most of the correlations between mean overinclusive scores and mean distraction effect scores were found to be significant.

McGhie and Chapman have carried out a number of experimental studies to examine some of the hypotheses yielded by their earlier (1961) clinical observations of attentional impairment in schizophrenic patients. Their basic technique has been to select tasks which involve specific areas of mental functioning and to examine the effect of various forms of distraction upon schizophrenic performance. Some of their investigations (Chapman and McGhie, 1962; McGhie, Chapman and Lawson, 1965a) have been concerned with the effect of experimentally imposed distraction upon the psychomotor performance of schizophrenic patients. For this purpose a battery of tests selected from Fleishman's (1954) standard psychomotor tasks was modified to allow the effect of both auditory and visual distraction to be examined independently. The battery was given to matched groups of schizophrenic patients, non-schizophrenic psychotic patients and a normal control group. In the absence of distraction, *all* psychotic patients showed a low level of psychomotor performance, this being in accordance with the findings of a variety of other studies (Shakow and Huston, 1936; King, 1954). When the tests were repeated with experimentally induced distraction, the performance of most patients deteriorated slightly but this decline was no more evident in the schizophrenic than in any other diagnostic group. The majority of the tests employed were simple speed tests involving a motor response to a predictable stimulus. In a few of the tests demanding the processing of unpredictable signals, distraction was found to have a significant and specific effect upon the performance of the schizophrenic patients. Thus, in a signal tracking task, involving the tracking of a variable visual signal, the level of schizophrenic performance fell sharply when either visual or auditory distracting stimuli were introduced.

In a later series of investigations (McGhie, Chapman and Lawson, 1965b; Lawson, McGhie and Chapman, 1967) the same workers examined the effect of distraction on tasks involving the processing, storage and recall of information. The main technique here was to present the patient with information, usually consisting of a series of rapidly presented letters or digits, together with a similar series of irrelevant information. The patient's task was to observe and report the relevant series, while ignoring the irrelevant information. In some of the tests the relevant and irrelevant information were both presented in the same sensory modality, while in others two sensory modalities were involved. Although the findings of these investigations confirmed the susceptibility of schizophrenic patients to distraction, they also indicated that this effect varied greatly with the nature of the task and with the sensory modalities involved. Compared with other psychotic patients, the schizophrenic group were seen to have considerable difficulty in coping with tasks which demanded the integration of information from two different sensory modalities. It was also noticeable that, when presented with a task of this nature the schizophrenic patient did most poorly in his processing of *visual* information. Furthermore, in a number of tasks requiring the perception and recall of either auditory or visual information, in the absence of distraction, schizophrenic patients showed themselves capable of processing auditory information reasonably well, but performed badly with an equivalent task in the visual modality. This suggestion, that schizophrenic patients are deficient in their processing of visual information, supported by a number of investigations reported by these workers, had been interpreted in the light of Sperling (1960) and Conrad's (1964) work on the normal processing of visual information. These studies suggest that visually presented data is normally recoded into an auditory form prior to storage. It is possible that this recoding process creates a further source of difficulty and causes the schizophrenic patient to be particularly poor in his performance on visual tasks. McGhie, Chapman and Lawson (1964, 1965) have also demonstrated the schizophrenic patient's difficulty with processing visual, as opposed to auditory, information is similar to that shown by elderly normal subjects. One of their current interests is in examining more directly the properties of the visual after-image and the rate at which schizophrenics are able to 'read-out' information from this brief visual store into the more stable auditory storage system.

The effect of distraction upon the performance of

schizophrenics in these simple tests of information processing was found to be relatively slight in the case of visual tasks. In such tasks the basic performance of schizophrenic patients was so low that it is possible that any effects of distraction would not be evident. However, on tasks requiring the processing of auditory information the effect of distraction on schizophrenic performance was very marked. These effects were independent of the sensory modality in which the distracting stimuli were presented. This finding of a modality specific effect of distraction on schizophrenic performance is again evident in a more recent investigation by the same team of workers (Lawson, McGhie and Chapman, 1967). The findings of these studies are summarized in Table 1.

Table 1
Schizophrenic Performance on Tasks Involving Processing of Auditory and Visual Information – With or Without Distraction.

Sensory modality of main task	*Sensory modality of distraction*	*Schizophrenic performance*
A+V	–	Poor
A	–	Good
V	–	Poor
A	A	High distraction effect
A	V	High distraction effect
V	A	No distraction effect
V	V	No distraction effect

A = Auditory V = Visual

These workers have interpreted their experimental findings in a model of disturbed attention which leans heavily on Broadbent's (1958) theory of a limited capacity decision channel. Studies of normal information processing have already made it clear that the limitation of the human communication channel is an informational one, so that the number of stimuli which can be responded to at any time is determined by the amount of information they contain. It is thus possible to deal with more than one set of data at a time only if the informational demands of each task are small. In order to function effectively, the individual is forced to perform a selective filtering operation on the input to ensure that his limited capacity is not overloaded. McGhie and his colleagues interpret their findings as indicating that in schizophrenia this normal filtering process has broken down so that the patients are less able to attend selectively and to process only relevant information. This defect may be expected to have varying effects depending upon the nature and demands of any task. In dealing with a situation requiring a response to simple predictable stimuli, overloading will be less likely and the patient's deficit less obvious. In tasks demanding the monitoring of a range of stimuli involving more complex decision making and fully occupying the limited decision channel, the failure in selective attention is more likely to lead to overloading and consequent breakdown in performance. In dealing with visual data the relatively slow rate of recoding information into the auditory modality increases the likelihood of overloading.

The communication difficulties, observed so clearly in schizophrenic patients, have focused a great deal of clinical interest upon the patient's inability to express his thoughts in speech and to assimilate in a meaningful way the speech of others. In spite of the clearly observable language deficiency of the schizophrenic, relatively few attempts have been made to systematically examine schizophrenic language disturbance. The majority of studies which have been reported have been concerned with a psycholinguistic analysis of the content of schizophrenic speech. In their first clinical study, McGhie and Chapman (1961) noted many examples of the patient's inability to process incoming verbal material and suggested that at least part of this deficiency could be regarded as a secondary consequence of the attentional deficit. The following extract is characteristic of the reports given by a number of young schizophrenic patients of their inability to comprehend the speech of others.

When people talk to me now it's like a different kind of language. It's too much to hold at once. My head is overloaded and I can't understand what they say. It makes you forget what you've just heard because you can't get hearing it long enough. It's all in different bits which you have to put together again in your head – just words in the air unless you can figure it out from their faces.

An examination of such reports suggested to these workers that the patient's difficulties arise, not from an inability to perceive the individual words comprising a connected discourse, but from an inability to perceive the words in meaningful relationship to each other as part of an organized pattern. Studies of normal speech (e.g. Shannon, 1951) have made it clear that speech processing is facilitated by the 'redundancy' in normal language structure. Such redundancy makes it possible for a passage of speech to be adequately comprehended without necessarily processing every word contained in it.

Investigations of normal subjects (Miller, 1963; Goldman-Eisler, 1961) suggest that speech is usually assimilated in phrase units of three to four words. Listening to speech is essentially a matter of making decisions about what is being said and storing these decisions in short-term memory to allow the communication to be subsequently understood in its entirety. Our ability to organize incoming speech into small phrase units ensures that, in listening to normal speech (at a rate of approximately 150 words per minute), the decision rate is reduced to a comfortable level (approximately one second), well within our capacity for processing information. The reports of schizophrenic patients suggest that their difficulty in assimilating speech is due both to a deficiency in the screening out of 'redundant' information, and to an inability to organize the incoming verbal data in an economical way.

As a preliminary test of this hypothesis Lawson, McGhie and Chapman presented schizophrenic patients, patients suffering from other psychiatric conditions, and normal subjects, with passages of English prose of different degrees of internal organization (Miller and Selfridge, 1950). These varied from collections of random, unrelated words (zero constraint) to standard English text. The intervening passages were graded according to the degree of contextual constraint involved in their structure. The results give clear indication that, although the schizophrenic patients were able to perceive and recall sentences of low contextual constraint as well as the controls, they fared badly in comparison with non-schizophrenics, in dealing with sentences of higher constraint (see Figure 7).

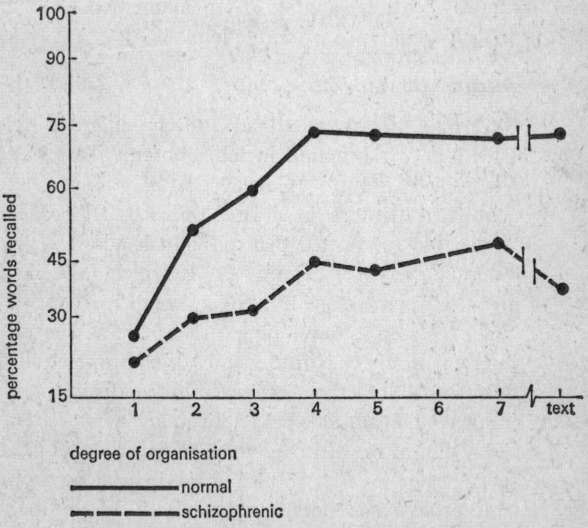

Figure 7 Variations of recall scores of schizophrenic and normal subjects on contextual constraint passages (Lawson et al., *1964)*

The schizophrenic patient seems unable to utilize the transitional bonds between words which normally facilitate our perception of the passage as an organized whole. By processing speech in single words rather than in phrase units, he requires to make decisions about what is being said at the rate of three to four per second. It was also theorized that, if the deficiency in speech perception of schizophrenic patients was due in part to an inability to screen out irrelevant information, there should be a direct connexion between poor performance on the speech test and a high distraction score on the previously mentioned tests of distraction. A high positive and significant correlation between these two measures was found (Lawson, 1965), and taken to support this interpretation that the poor speech perception of some schizophrenic patients was a consequence of a breakdown in selective attention. Laffal (1961) has applied a similar method of analysis to schizophrenic speech production.

Attention and cognitive control

Silverman has proposed an entirely different theory of attentional dysfunction in schizophrenia, based upon the Menninger group's (Gardner *et al.*, 1959) studies of cognitive attitudes in normal subjects. The Menninger studies have indicated that individuals adopt certain consistent patterns of cognitive style which influence broad areas of their behaviour. Such 'cognitive control' principles are seen as developing early in life as a result of the interaction of constitutional and environmental forces. Once established they become enduring dispositions which influence the subject's behaviour in a wide variety of situations. Cognitive attitudes may be regarded as individual strategies or ways of co-ordinating private perceptual and conceptual experiences in dealing with the external world. Among the various cognitive control principles which have been delineated by Gardner and others are two which are specifically related to the attentive process. One of these – *scanning control* – reflects differences in the extensiveness with which stimuli are sampled when attention is directed to any perceptual field. The other attentive principle of cognitive control – *field articulation* – refers to differences in attending to complex perceptual fields and particularly to the inhibition of other non-essential aspects of the perceptual field. Factor analysis of scores on tests measuring scanning control and field articulation principles (Gardner, 1961) has indicated that these two cognitive control principles are independent measures of attentional behaviour. The first of these two factors, scanning control, is an elaboration of Piaget's (1961) discussion of the development of attention in the young child. Piaget's work indicated that early in development the young child tends to fixate dominant objects in the stimulus field and that this causes him to overestimate the stimuli in the centre of the visual field. This centration effect is used to explain over- and underestimations of the distance of objects in the centre or periphery of the perceptual field. Such errors in judgement of apparent size or distance have been found to be related to the amount of time during which the subjects '*centre*' upon the stimuli in the course of making their judgements. Long durations of centrations (extensive scanning) have been shown to be related to underestimation of the stimulus, while minimal scanning is associated with overestimation of the stimulus.

Silverman (1964a and b) surveyed a number of perceptual studies of effect of schizophrenic patients to suggest that deteriorated chronic schizophrenics (excluding those with paranoid symptomatology) show a constant tendency towards low scores on Gardner's scanning factor. These patients may then be described as *minimal scanners*. The second of the two attentional factors, *field articulation*, measures the ability to direct attention selectively to one of two conflicting sets of cues. Silverman's survey of studies using tests purporting to measure field articulation demonstrates that the chronic (non-paranoid) schizophrenic shows a strong tendency towards undifferentiated and poor field articulation. In contrast to other theories which have suggested that the schizophrenic is overwhelmed with stimulation at a rate which he cannot handle, possibly as a result of a breakdown in the filtering mechanism of the reticular activating system, Silverman views him as *actively* monitoring out stimulation to defend himself against a hostile environment. Silverman turns to the early social experiences of the schizophrenic patients to find explanations for the defensive system which later corrupts the attentive process. Thus, Silverman's theory lines up with other theories such as Bannister's *serial invalidation hypothesis* (1962) which regard schizophrenia as a product of intrapsychic conflict and repeated environmental trauma. However, it is impossible to do justice to Silverman's theory while still approaching schizophrenia as a single entity. An essential feature of Silverman's model of the schizophrenic deficit is the clear distinction drawn between paranoid and non-paranoid schizophrenic patients (see page 91).

Mental set

Few psychologists have studied schizophrenia more intensively than Shakow who has devoted some fifty years of experimental research to this problem. It is impossible to give adequate cover to the wide-ranging experimental studies reported by Shakow and his colleagues and we shall restrict ourselves to a summary of some of his findings which have direct relevance to attentional dysfunction in schizophrenia. Shakow (1963) has shown that a common feature of schizophrenic performance in a variety of experimental studies is that schizophrenic patients tend to do poorly in situations involving voluntary behaviour, where the activity is experimenter-controlled. In tasks such as tapping and steadiness tests where the activity, although often complex, is self-initiated the schizophrenic patient performs at a much higher level. Another general feature of the schizophrenic patient's experimental behaviour is what Shakow terms a 'neo-phobia'.

Curiosity and search for stimulation seem particularly weak in the schizophrenic. He appears to suffer from the kind of neophobia I have alluded to ... the disturbance that results from entry into new settings, from contact with the uncertain. He seems to prefer old, already experienced situations. His lack of involvement with his environment, seen for example in his poor cooperation, is another aspect of this deficit. When given the choice he prefers superficial to demanding tasks; he neither resumes tasks after interruption, nor utilizes substitute tasks to deal with the tensions presumably created by incompletion (Shakow, 1966).

Shakow's work has illustrated how this behaviour is reflected in the schizophrenic patient's performance in a number of different types of learning situations where he is particularly affected in the early part of the learning series (Huston and Shakow, 1948, 1949). In contrast to this, if he is allowed to work on without interruption this difficulty gradually recedes and his performance improves (Huston and Shakow, 1949). His poor adaptiveness is also apparent in other situations calling for no overt responses other than at the autonomic level. Thus, in a series of studies of autonomic adaptability involving measurements of galvanic skin response, heart rate, and other responses effected through repeated presentation of stimuli, the schizophrenic patient adapts autonomically at a much slower rate than non-schizophrenic subjects. When heart rate is measured in response to pain stimulations given at regular intervals, the heart rate of the schizophrenic patient does not show the same diminution as that of normal subjects (Cohen and Patterson, 1937). Similarly in a G.S.R. (galvanic skin response) study of orienting reactions to visual and auditory stimuli, schizophrenic patients did not show the normal progressive adaptation to the auditory and visual stimuli, tending to remain throughout at a significantly higher level of arousal (Zahn, Rosenthal and Lawlor, 1963).

Many of Shakow's ideas on the schizophrenic deficit have been gathered from repeated studies of the reaction-time performance of these patients. In accordance with others who have utilized this procedure, Shakow finds that schizophrenic patients demonstrate considerably slower simple reaction times than other patients and normal subjects (Huston, Shakow and Riggs, 1937). Normal performance on reaction time improves if the subject is aware that the preparatory interval (the period between the warning signal and the stimulus) is regular and therefore predictable. Shakow's work illustrates that the schizophrenic patient is unable to take advantage of this predictability to improve his performance unless the preparatory interval is a very brief one (not more than six seconds). He is also greatly affected by the immediately preceding interval so that when a series of longer preparatory intervals, giving longer reaction times, precedes a series of shorter ones, his reaction times for the shorter series are markedly lengthened (Zahn, Rosenthal and Shakow, 1961). In a choice reaction-time situation the performance of the schizophrenic patient is significantly affected by the presence of irrelevant stimuli which do not evoke a response. In one of these reaction-time studies (Rodnick and Shakow, 1940) a 'set index' was developed, based upon lengths of reaction times and their relationship between regular and irregular preparatory periods. This index successfully differentiated schizophrenic and normal groups without any degree of overlap.

Shakow and his colleagues have interpreted the set index as a reliable measure of the patient's inability to maintain a required mental set. It has been suggested by Knehr (1954) that the set index in reaction-time studies is contaminated by intelligence and that differences in the set index between schizophrenic and non-schizophrenic subjects may merely reflect the lower intellectual level of the former group. This possibility was considered by Tizard and Venables (1956) who repeated the Rodnick and Shakow experiment with groups of schizophrenics, normals and a group of intellectual subnormal adults. Their results tend to refute Knehr's criticism, in that the subnormal subject's set indices were comparable to that of the normal subjects, while those of the schizophrenic patients were significantly reduced. Later the Worcester group (Rosenthal, Lawlor, Zahn and Shakow, 1960) found no correlation between the set index and a performance test of intelligence but a highly significant positive correlation between the index and a rating of schizophrenic disorganization.

A further examination of some of the factors influencing the mental set of schizophrenic patients in the reaction-time situation is contained in another study of the Worcester group (Cromwell, Rosenthal, Shakow and Zahn, 1961). This investigation introduced three different conditions of controlling the length of the preparatory interval before the presentation of the reaction-time signal. Under the first (autonomy) condition the subject was allowed to decide his own preparatory interval while under the second (control) condition the subject was informed of the length of the interval but the onset of the preparatory signal was under the control of the investigator. In the final (controlled-blind) condition the preparatory signal was controlled completely by the experimenter without the subject's knowledge. The results of a comparison of the reaction-time performance of groups of schizophrenic and normal subjects under the different conditions is illustrated in Figure 8.

It can be seen that, whereas normal subjects improve their performance under the self-initiated autonomy conditions, the schizophrenic patients produce their faster reaction times under completely externally controlled conditions. Some workers (e.g. Hunt and Cofer, 1944) have suggested that the results of most reaction-time studies may simply reflect the inadequate cooperation of the schizophrenic patient and his reduced responsiveness to social stimulation. On this argument the primary deficit would be regarded as motivational rather than a cognitive attentional deficit affecting attention. A somewhat similar view has been put by Morris (1963) who has criticized the

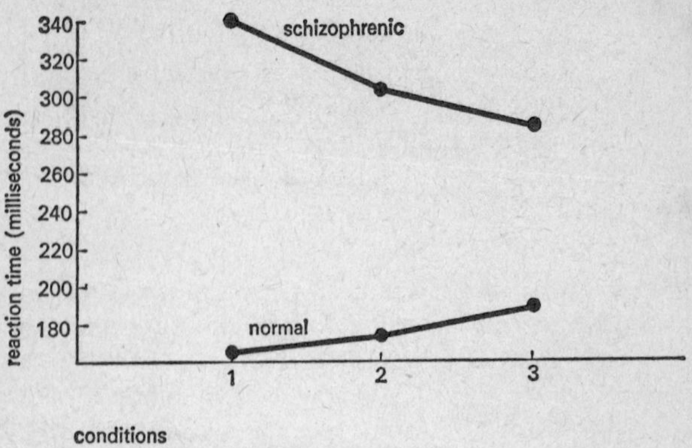

Figure 8 Reaction time as a function of experimental conditions (Cromwell et al., *1961)*

assumption made by McGhie and Chapman (1961) that the reports of their schizophrenic patients refer only to disturbed attention. In her own similar study she finds that the reports of schizophrenic patients suggest a disturbance of what she terms *intentional* as well as attentional behaviour. Intentional behaviour refers to reduced volition, poor responsiveness to social stimulation and a general low level of motivation.

Shakow (1963) has put forward a model of the schizophrenic deficit which embraces disturbances in both attentional and intentional behaviour. He suggests that the schizophrenic is impaired in his ability to maintain *major sets* so that his behaviour is controlled by a number of independent and isolated *segmental sets*. Goldstein and Sheerer (1941) have already referred to the schizophrenic patient's inability to hold the mental set required to maintain an adequate state of readiness to respond to stimuli. Shakow's concept of major or generalized sets is a more complex one involving some aspects of Coghill's theory of integrated action and Cameron's concept of homeostasis. He suggests that one of the main functions of the cortex is to control, integrate and organize current input and past experience in such a way as to produce goal-directed, integrated behaviour. In the schizophrenic patient, the failure of the central mechanism to control and integrate input results in areas of behaviour being segmentalized or dissociated, and thus functioning independently. One effect of this lack of integration is that he becomes preoccupied with the mechanics of processes rather than with their unified ends:

> There is increased awareness and preoccupation with the ordinarily disregarded details of existence – the details which normal people spontaneously forget, train themselves, or get trained rigorously to disregard. He (the schizophrenic) is, as in the case of the centipede of the fable, so deeply concerned about the way his feet move that he loses sight of where they should be going (Shakow, 1963).

Shakow does not speculate directly on the possible causes of this breakdown in integration although at times he would appear to favour a psychodynamic view of schizophrenic aetiology. Thus, he refers to the schizophrenic maintaining minor sets '... in an indirect effort to obtain the satisfaction of primitive, fundamental needs, which, in contrast with the normal person, have never been adequately satisfied. ... Integrated control is therefore abandoned and the automatically matured devices are pervertedly used to satisfy the needs' (Shakow, 1966). At other times his writings infer that the schizophrenic deficit is a result of cortical disturbance resulting in an inability to control and organize behaviour in a purposeful manner. In discussing the failure of cortical integration, Shakow's explanatory theory comes close to that put forward by McGhie and his colleagues, although it is based upon a quite different set of findings:

> It is as if, in the scanning process which takes place before the response to a stimulus is made, the schizophrenic is unable to select out the material relevant for optimal response. He apparently cannot free himself from the irrelevant among the numerous possibilities available for choice. In other words, that function which is of equal importance is a response *to*

stimuli, namely the protection *against* the response to stimuli, is abeyant (Shakow, 1962).

Later he goes on to comment that:

these irrelevant associations to which the normal is also subject but to a much lesser degree would appear to arise from three sources: chance distractors from the environment; irrelevancies from the stimulus situation; and irrelevancies from past experience ... the mere presence of these irrelevant factors ... seems to lead the schizophrenic to give them focal rather than ground significance, signal rather noise import (Shakow, 1962).

A rather different approach to measuring the mental set of schizophrenic patients is that based upon Uznadze's concept of *fixated set* and developed by Soviet psychologists in their studies of schizophrenia. In a recent paper Bzhalava (1965) utilized this technique in a comparative study of epileptic and schizophrenic patients. The initial procedure involves placing two balls of markedly different size on the open hand of blindfold subjects and requesting them to indicate which hand holds the larger ball. If repeated rehearsals of this procedure are followed by the presentation of balls of equal size, it is found that most subjects will continue for some time to perceive the balls as being of unequal size. Continued presentation of the equal balls ultimately results in an abandonment of this fixated set and a regaining of correct perception. The number of presentations of equal stimuli required to extinguish the formerly established mental set provides a measure of its strength. The procedure may also be repeated in other modalities using for example tachistoscopic presentations of circles to examine fixation of set in the visual modality. With epileptic patients Bzhalava found that a strongly fixated set was established in the tactile modality but only a small minority of patients showed a fixated set in the visual modality. However, in schizophrenic patients a fixated set was easily and quickly established in either modality. Furthermore, once a fixated set is established to stimuli in one modality it is immediately transferred to stimuli in any other modality without additional rehearsal in the second modality. It was also found that schizophrenics automatically generalized their fixated set to alternative pairs of objects presented in the same modality. Thus, a set quickly established to perceive two equal circles as unequal was carried over when the patient was subsequently presented with pairs of lines or triangles. This diffuseness of sensory adaptation of the schizophrenic patients is interpreted by Bzhalava (1965) as indicative of volitional impairment:

> The patient strives to dispense with the necessity of having recourse to a volitional act required for the overcoming of an experimentally set-up difficulty. . . . A clear impression is produced that for schizophrenics, fixation of *intention* is unattainable, i.e. they cannot be brought to act on the basis of a specifically volitional set and thus to switch over from the first level of activity to the second.

This type of inability to switch from one mental set to another has been observed in other studies of schizophrenic performance. Huston, Cohen and Senf (1955) found that schizophrenic subjects had great difficulty in shifting attention between different types of tasks under different conditions of distraction. Their observations led them to conclude that the fixated set of schizophrenics was more evident in situations demanding the shifting of attention between stimuli open to personal and social interpretations, and less evident in more objective tasks (e.g. arithmetical calculations).

While it is thus well established that schizophrenic patients have difficulty in maintaining or shifting required mental sets, it is less certain whether this deficit is a consequence of cognitive or motivational disorder.

Sustained attention

As an inability to sustain attention over a period of time has often been observed to be a characteristic feature of the clinical picture of schizophrenia, it might be expected that vigilance studies would be a rewarding area of research. That there have been very few systematic investigations of schizophrenic vigilance performance, may possibly reflect the acceptance of the fact that such patients are less likely to be motivated highly enough to co-operate on such relatively lengthy tasks. One of the few reports of research in this area are those by Claridge (1960, 1967) using a psychotic group composed mainly of schizophrenic patients. Claridge used an auditory vigilance task consisting of a thirty-minute recording of random digits read out at the rate of one per second. The signals to be detected were runs of three consecutive odd digits. His results are illustrated in Figure 9.

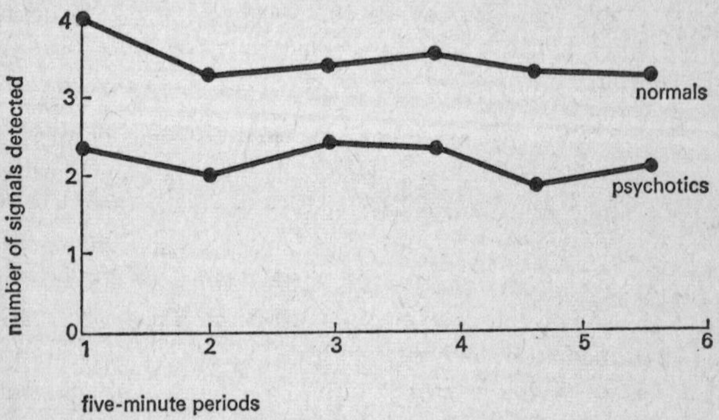

Figure 9 Auditory vigilance curves for psychotic and normal subjects (Claridge, 1967)

The overall vigilance performance of the mixed psychotic group was significantly inferior to that of the normal subjects. However, there was a much higher scatter of scores in the psychotic group, where the variance estimate was exactly twice that of the normals.

That this heterogeneity was not altogether due to the mixture of schizophrenic and manic-depressive patients in the psychotic group was evident in Claridge's breakdown of the schizophrenic subjects into diagnostic subcategories, but this will be considered in a later section of this chapter.

Vigilance performance has frequently been accepted as an indirect measure of arousal level on the grounds that a falling rate of signal detection is due to reduced arousal consequent upon the monotonous conditions of the task. Such studies therefore link up with the growing number of investigations of variations in arousal level in schizophrenia.

Arousal level

Investigations of the arousal level of schizophrenic patients have been well reviewed by Venables (1966), and, more extensively by Claridge (1967). This discussion will be limited to a brief summary of the results of some studies which have a particular bearing upon attentional deficit in schizophrenia.

Although E.E.G. studies of schizophrenic patients have produced discouragingly ambiguous results, agreement has been reached that fast or choppy records are characteristic of some schizophrenic patients (e.g. Davis and Davis, 1939). Such E.E.G. findings have suggested that some schizophrenic patients function at an abnormally high level of cortical activation. Another quantitative measure of E.E.G. activity is the variability of the E.E.G. record. There is some evidence to suggest that the coefficient of variability of the integrated E.E.G. is inversely related to the level of activation. In two E.E.G. studies Goldstein and his colleagues (1963, 1965) found that the average coefficient of variation of electrical energy in the E.E.G. was much lower for chronic schizophrenics than for normals, thus adding support to the idea that some forms of schizophrenia are characterized by a high level of cortical activation.

Further indirect support for this suggestion comes

from the work of Mirsky and his colleagues in the U.S.A. (1960). Mirsky has utilized a signal-detection task developed by Rosvold *et al.* (1956) as a means of measuring variations of attention in brain-damaged patients. This test, the Continuous Performance Test (C.P.T.) employs the visual presentation, by means of a revolving drum, of single letters, briefly exposed one at a time through a small aperture. The test has two conditions, the first requiring the subject to respond by key-pressing only when the letter X is exposed and the second requiring a response only when the X appears following an A. Previous use of this test in the assessment of brain-damaged patients had already suggested that performance on the C.P.T. is particularly vulnerable to damage to the mid-brain centres which are thought to mediate arousal. Further support for this interpretation was given by Kornetsky and Mirsky's (1966) finding that drugs such as chlorpromazine, which are known to act upon the mid-brain reticular system, directly affect performance on the C.P.T. The Wechsler Digit Symbol Substitution Test (D.S.S.T.) was selected by Mirsky as representing a task dependent upon cortical, but independent of sub-cortical, mid-brain structures. The validity of this contrast between these two tests is supported by Kornetsky and Mirsky's (1966) study which showed that moderate doses of barbiturates, known to act mainly at a cortical level, impair the performance on the D.S.S.T. and not on the C.P.T. On the basis of such inferences from previous findings it was postulated that schizophrenic patients would do badly on the C.P.T. but reasonably well on the D.S.S.T. which does not depend upon arousal level for its execution. This was confirmed by Orzack and Kornetsky (1966) and their results would appear to offer further support to the hypothesis that the schizophrenic patient is over-aroused. However, Orzack and Kornetsky noted that this indirect evidence of a higher level of activation was true only of some schizophrenic patients, others displaying no such signs of high arousal levels. These and other differences found within the schizophrenic group will be considered in more detail in a later part of this discussion.

Another indirect method of assessing the level of cortical activation level is based on the earlier finding (Lindsley, 1958) that the ability to differentiate a pair of light flashes presented in close temporal proximity increases with a heightening of the level of activation. This relationship between the threshold of fusion of paired light flashes and cortical activation has been used by some workers in a number of psychophysiological studies of schizophrenia. Venables and Wing (1962) were able to show that schizophrenic patients had a high level of fusion for paired light flashes. Their findings also indicated a positive association between the two-flash threshold and clinical ratings of the degree of social withdrawal of psychiatric patients. Later, similar results were found employing paired auditory clicks in the place of light flashes (Venables, 1967). These findings indicate that the more withdrawn schizophrenic patient is at a higher level of cortical activation. This might suggest that the social withdrawal of the schizophrenic patient is a defensive reaction aimed at limiting stimulation and reducing arousal level.

Another test which has been taken to provide an indirect measure of the level of cortical activation is the spiral after-effect (S.A.E.). When a rotating spiral is fixated for some time it produces an after-effect of apparent movement in the opposite direction. This visual illusion has been for long of interest to psychologists interested in perceptual anomalies and recently a detailed review of its use has been published by Holland (1965). Its main interest to clinical psychologists has been its application in measuring changes due to brain damage but more recently it has been employed as a correlative measure of arousal. Several investigations have found a significant correlation between the S.A.E. and alpha blocking, suggesting that longer after-effects are indicative of high arousal levels (Claridge and Herrington, 1963).

The application of the S.A.E. to schizophrenic patients has produced conflicting results. Whereas some studies (e.g. Price and Deabler, 1955) have found no differences between schizophrenic and normal groups, others (e.g. Herrington and Claridge, 1965) have reported a significantly longer after-effect in schizophrenic patients. In a more recent investigation, using a larger group of sixty-seven psychotic patients (all but five of whom were schizophrenic), Claridge (1967) replicated his previous findings which support the hypothesis of a higher level of arousal in schizophrenia. It is of some interest to note that all Claridge's patients, including those examined in his previous investigations, were at the acute stage of their illness and that there is therefore no evidence of increased S.A.E. in chronic schizophrenia.

The hypothesis that the duration of spiral after-effect may represent an indirect measure of arousal level should, however, be viewed with some caution. In his review of the literature on the spiral after-effect, Holland (1965) raises the possibility that variations in the effect may reflect more superficial aspects of behaviour such as eye movement rate or the ability to fixate the moving spiral. The findings of a recent investigation, using the spiral after-effect with brain-damaged subjects (Efstathiou and Morant, 1966), suggest that failure to experience the effect may be due to inattentiveness rather than to the influence of any specific neurological damage on the experience of movement after-effect.

Variations in the level of automatic activity have also been used as measures of arousal level. Level of skin potential has been shown to give reliable measures of arousal in normal groups and this technique has been applied by Venables and Wing (1962) to schizophrenic patients. The results of this study indicated not only that the (chronic) schizophrenic patients show a high arousal level but also that the skin conductance measures are correlated with clinical ratings of social withdrawal. The only exception to this association occurs with paranoid patients. These findings support the suggestion of the two-flash threshold measure of arousal that withdrawn patients are at a high level of arousal (see Figure 10).

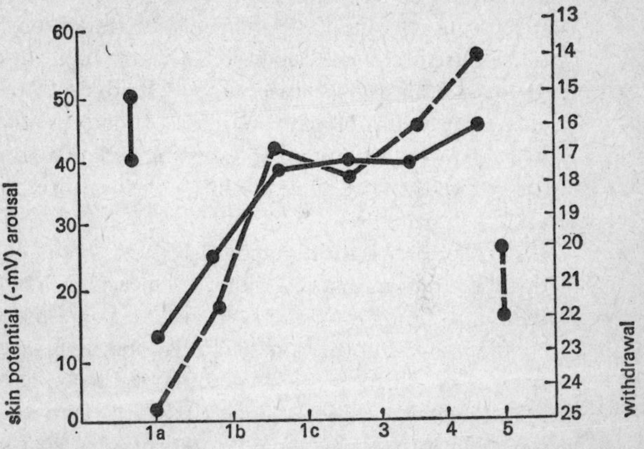

Figure 10 Relationship between measures of arousal and withdrawal in chronic schizophrenic patients (Venables and Wing, 1962). (Numbers on the horizontal axis refer to different clinical sub-groups)

Sedation threshold level has also been used fairly extensively as a measure of activation level (Shagass, 1954). This is measured by giving the patient intravenous injections of sodium amytal until his speech is slurred, until he fails to respond to certain tests of attention, or until a criterion level of E.E.G. activity is reached. The dosage of sodium amytal required to reach this point is indicative of the original arousal level of the patient. Claridge (1967) has shown that the sedation thresholds are consistently related to other measures of autonomic reactivity, such as heart rate and blood pressure response to drugs affecting the autonomic nervous system. Most investigations which have used the sedation threshold measure of arousal with schizophrenic patients report abnormally low levels (indicating an under-aroused state) in acutely ill patients.

Shagass, who originally developed the technique, reported (1960) that acute schizophrenics who had been ill for less than six months had the lowest sedation thresholds of any clinical group studied. In this and other studies (e.g. Krishnamoorti and Shagass, 1964) more chronically ill schizophrenics were reported to have high thresholds (indicating an over-aroused state). Claridge's (1967) study of a large group of schizophrenic patients used a somewhat different technique of assessing sedation thresholds but arrived at the same findings of low thresholds for acutely ill patients.

As there is much in common between both the operational definitions and techniques of measuring the arousal level and the orienting response as used in Russian psychology, any information on variations of orienting responses in schizophrenics would appear to be relevant to the present issue. Most of the Russian work reports that the majority of schizophrenic patients are characterized by a weakness or absence of the orienting response, indicating a low arousal level. Studies by Stretslova (1955), based mainly on measurement of variations of pupil dilation under stimulation, found that around two-thirds of the schizophrenics examined gave weak or absent orienting responses. Other investigations (e.g. Traugott, Balenov, Kauffman and Luchko, 1958) report reduced orienting responses of schizophrenic patients to a variety of visual, and auditory and tactile stimuli. However, most of these workers have also noted that some schizophrenic patients show unusually strong orienting responses which are difficult to extinguish.

The findings on the arousal level of schizophrenic patients are complicated by the somewhat ambiguous nature of the concept of arousal itself and particularly by the variety of techniques used in its assessment. Some workers (e.g. Sternbach, 1960) have found no association between E.E.G. measures of cortical arousal and other measures of autonomic reactivity in normal subjects. Hume and Claridge (1965) found only a slight and insignificant positive correlation between autonomic arousal as measured by skin potential and a two-flash threshold measure of cortical arousal.

In contrast to this Venables (1963) has found a *negative* correlation between skin potential and two-flash threshold measures of arousal in normal subjects. Other workers (Darrow, Pathman and Kronenberg, 1946; Stennett, 1957) suggest that the association between autonomic and E.E.G. activity may depend on the existing arousal level, positive correlations between the two being more likely at high levels of arousal. It would therefore appear unwise at this stage to readily equate results of investigations using different measurements of arousal as if they represented a unified measure of one specific arousal process.

The interrelation of arousal measures in schizophrenic patients is perhaps even more ambiguous. Venables (1963) has found that the skin potential and paired light-flash thresholds are positively associated in schizophrenic subjects in contrast to his own findings with normal subjects where he reports a dissociation between these two aspects of arousal. Venables (1967) suggests that these findings might be interpreted to suggest that in some (more chronic) schizophrenic patients, autonomic and cortical systems of arousal operate in parallel, cortical activity not being controlled by the normal regulatory action of the reticular system. In this view the schizophrenic patient is seen to suffer from an inability to control selectively his responsiveness to significant stimuli, resulting in an indiscriminate arousal reaction to all stimuli.

Claridge (1967) has used the distinction between cortical and autonomic measures of arousal in a somewhat different way to produce a more comprehensive psychophysiological model of arousal. The model proposed by Claridge involves two functionally related arousal mechanisms which he terms the *tonic arousal system* and the *arousal modulating system*. The function of the former tonic system is to maintain the individual's overall level of arousal while the second modulating system regulates the activity level of the tonic arousal system and guards the central nervous system from overstimulation. Apart from this homeostatic role, the modulating system also filters incoming information to facilitate the reception of relevant and inhibit the reception of irrelevant data. Claridge's diagnostic representation of the two linked systems is illustrated in Figure 11.

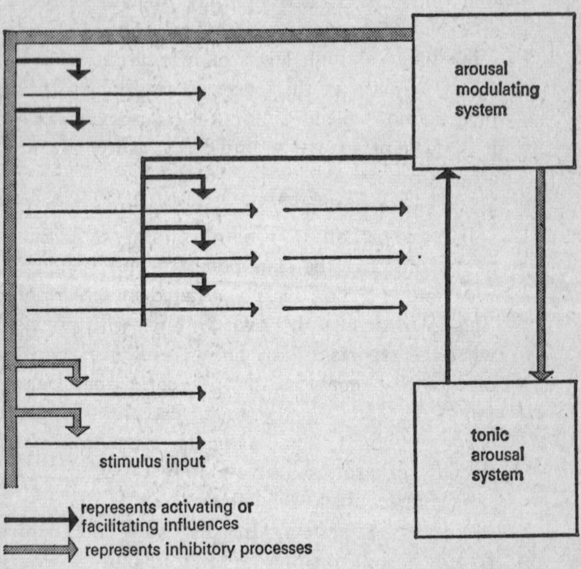

Figure 11 Dual arousal model (Claridge, 1967)

It is postulated that, in schizophrenia the two systems become functionally dissociated due to a breakdown in the feed-back mechanisms preserving the normal balance. The effects of such imbalance will depend upon which of the two systems are predominant in their function. If the dissociation results in a weakening of the modulating system, disinhibition of the tonic system would cause an abnormally high level of arousal. As incoming information would no longer be effectively monitored, attention would become less selective and directed in its operation. However, if imbalance resulted in a weakening of the tonic system and strengthening of the modulating system's functions, arousal level would fall and attention would become severely narrowed.

This model helps to clarify the conflicting and often contradictory findings that schizophrenic patients are over- or under-aroused. In this formulation all schizophrenics suffer from both high and low levels of arousal, depending upon the arousal components being considered. Although the two systems are obvious parallels to the cortical and sub-cortical centres proposed in neurophysiological models, Claridge wisely refuses to use such terms on the grounds that they would imply a localization of function which would be out of context in a model based upon psychophysiological findings. While Claridge's dual arousal model has a certain theoretical appeal in its ability to resolve some of the hitherto discrepant findings, much of his evidence is based on the rather tenuous association between the spiral after-effect and cortical arousal.

Claridge's model of disturbed arousal in schizophrenia reflects once more the theme which has constantly intruded into our consideration of all the studies of attentional behaviour in schizophrenia. Most investigations of schizophrenic patients have stressed the high variance of performance within the schizophrenic population. Indeed, much of the ambiguity inherent in the diverse findings we have examined would appear to be a consequence of approaching the schizophrenic population as a relatively homogeneous group. Perhaps the most significant and useful contribution to be made by recent psychological studies has been their stressing of the heterogeneous nature of schizophrenia and their attempts to employ their findings to clarify its sub-classification. In the following section we will consider to what extent psychological studies of disturbed attention have achieved this aim of reducing the schizophrenic category to its more manageable component parts.

Variations in Attention Within the Schizophrenic Group

The original scheme of sub-classification put forward by Kraepelin (1896) and developed by Bleuler (1911) has been subject to much criticism. Of the four original sub-categories it is only the paranoid and hebephrenic forms of the illness which have really stood the test of time and are still regarded as a useful grouping. The clear-cut clinical differences between the paranoid schizophrenic and all other schizophrenic patients has led many workers to adopt the dichotomy of paranoid as opposed to non-paranoid forms of schizophrenia as one of the most reliable and valuable methods of demarcating within the schizophrenic group. In Kraepelin's original classification the paranoid group were viewed as a distinct diagnostic class under the term *paraphrenia* (1896). It was later included within schizophrenia when it was found that many patients previously diagnosed by Kraepelin as paraphrenic later developed clear schizophrenic symptoms. Later Kahlbaum suggested that the term *paranoia* be reserved for patients showing a chronic systematized delusional state, in the absence of other typical schizophrenic symptoms. However, so few cases of pure paranoia were found that the term fell into disrepute. Subsequent clinical studies have established that paranoid patients share so many common features in the history of their illness and in its current symptomatology, that many psychiatrists regard them as constituting a completely separate diagnostic category.

Another method of sub-dividing schizophrenia is denoted by two terms, *process* and *reactive* schizophrenia. The process category is applied to patients who show a poorly integrated, usually schizoid pre-psychotic personality, an insidious onset to their illness and a poor prognosis regardless of treatment. In contrast, the reactive category is applied to patients who have a relatively good pre-morbid personality, whose illness has shown a rapid, acute onset and whose prognosis is relatively good. Most workers who have applied the process-reactive dimension to schizophrenia have laid great weight on the pre-morbid personality of the patient, suggesting that the more malignant nature of the process schizophrenia is reflected in the patient's life-long inability to make an adequate adjustment to his environment.

The process-reactive dimension has some similarity to Langfeldt's (1939) distinction between 'true' or 'nuclear' schizophrenia and the '*schizophreniform*' psychosis, the latter term being applied to patients whose illness is less severe and runs a more benign course than that of the classical schizophrenic illness. In a follow-up study of a mixed group of patients (Eitinger, Laane and Langfeldt, 1958) it was shown that whereas only 50 per cent of these patients diagnosed as schizophrenic were eventually able to lead a normal independent social life, 75 per cent of those diagnosed as schizophreniform subsequently reached this criterion.

It is also clear that the concept of process schizophrenia has much in common with the original Kraepelinian subcategory of hebephrenia and it is doubtful whether the term adds much more to our knowledge. Nevertheless, it may be useful to separate out from the total schizophrenic group those patients whose symptoms suggest that they suffer from a more malignant or *nuclear* form of the illness corresponding to the original notion of dementia praecox. It may be that what is termed reactive schizophrenia is itself a heterogeneous group containing a mixture of conditions which require to be distinguished from the classical form of schizophrenia. A few years ago Slater and Beard (1963), reporting on their comparative study of schizophrenia and some forms of epileptic psychosis concluded:

> One might take the view that for schizophrenia we are now approaching the stage of understanding which was reached half a century ago with epilepsy. It was customary then to classify the epilepsies into idiopathic and symptomatic types, and in the latter case to specify the underlying condition of

which the epilepsy was symptomatic. This rather primitive stage in sub-classification may now become possible in the syndrome we call schizophrenia. Very likely the bulk of the cases so diagnosed will prove to be idiopathic, with genetic factors responsible for the specificities. But round this nucleus we would aim to define, with increasing precision, groups of cases in which the schizophrenia-like psychosis was traceable to known processes.

One might feel that the process or nuclear forms of schizophrenia come closest to Slater's concept of idiopathic schizophrenia.

A third division of the schizophrenic group divides patients according to the length of their illness, into the two categories of *acute* and *chronic*. Since Brown (1960) showed that schizophrenics are significantly less likely to improve after a continuous stay in hospital of two years or more, most research workers have adopted the two year hospital period as a convenient although arbitrary method of denoting the onset of chronicity. This method of categorization is rendered more significant by the suggestion in some research findings that the chronic form of the illness is not simply a worsening of the acute stage. There is some evidence that those patients who subsequently reach the chronic stage display qualitative differences in symptoms from patients whose illness terminates in the acute stage.

There is obviously a great deal of overlapping among the three systems of classification to which we have referred. Process schizophrenic patients, with their poorer response to treatment will be more likely to spend considerable time in hospital and thus be categorized as chronic patients. The non-paranoid category will include patients with hebephrenic symptoms, whose condition is more likely to run a chronic course. While it is thus clear that the different sub-categories are by no means independent of each other, it may be nevertheless profitable to examine the disturbances of attention of patients categorized within these crude classifications.

Paranoid and non-paranoid comparisons

After his preliminary studies of overinclusive thinking in undifferentiated schizophrenic groups Payne (1961) became interested in the possible association between overinclusive thinking and delusional formation:

> Overinclusive thinking could produce an extension of the boundaries of concepts in such a way that two normally mutually exclusive categories or concepts would overlap, containing elements in common. Thus, for the normal person, while the only possibilities are 'either'/'or', the overinclusive person can also conclude 'both'. ... In one sense, both overinclusive thinking and delusions are ... unwarranted generalizations from the data ... Thus the development of an extensive paranoid reaction could well be partly a function of overinclusive thinking.

In order to test this hypothesis, Payne, Caird and Laverty (1964) gave a test of overinclusive thinking to groups of deluded (paranoid) schizophrenics, non-deluded (non-paranoid) schizophrenics, and non-schizophrenic patient controls. Although the deluded schizophrenic patients were found to give high overinclusive scores which successfully differentiated them from the non-schizophrenic patients, no significant difference was found between the overinclusive scores of the deluded and non-deluded schizophrenic groups. Payne explained these results by assuming that some of his non-deluded patients who gave high overinclusive scores may have been secretly deluded.

In a more recent investigation (Payne and Caird, 1967), further evidence has been produced to support Payne's contention that overinclusion is associated with paranoid schizophrenias. We have already described the basic methodology of this investigation in discussing the effect of distraction on reaction-time performance (see pp. 56–7). In the first part of this study Payne and Caird presented findings in support of their hypothesis that the effect of various distracting conditions on reaction-time responses is greater for overinclusive as opposed to non-overinclusive schizophrenics. In a subsequent experiment these workers developed their earlier suggestion that over-inclusion is associated with paranoid symptomatology by comparing the performance of paranoid and non-paranoid patients on the distraction conditions. The results of these experiments are illustrated in Figure 12.

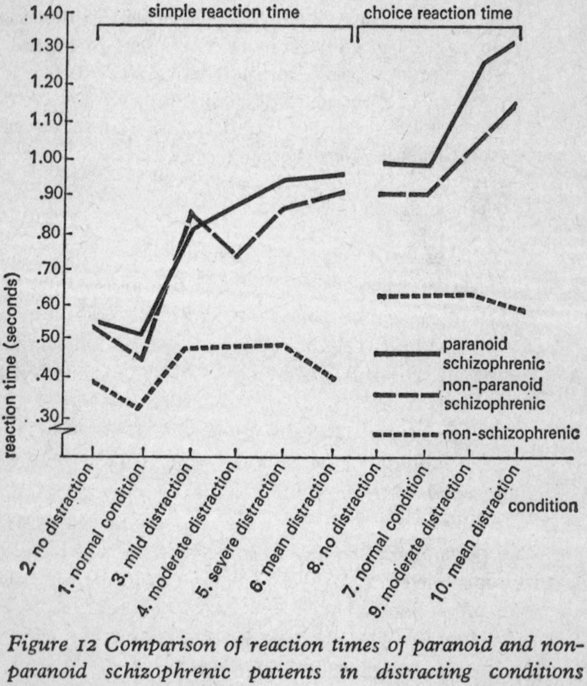

Figure 12 Comparison of reaction times of paranoid and non-paranoid schizophrenic patients in distracting conditions (Payne and Caird, 1967)

In spite of the significant trend of the mean scores, an analysis of variance carried out separately in the simple and choice reaction-time scores failed to confirm the significance of the interaction between paranoid diagnosis and distraction effect. Payne and Caird considered that the failure of this analysis to fully support their hypothesis was probably due to the heterogeneity of the non-paranoid group and repeated the analysis without this group. On this occasion the relevant interactions were significant, thus supporting their view that paranoid schizophrenia is associated with high distractibility and overinclusiveness. However, the high variance of the non-paranoid group scores suggests that some non-paranoid schizophrenic patients were more distractible than some patients with a paranoid diagnosis.

As overinclusive thinking has been related to a breakdown in the selective and inhibitory functions of attention this would imply that attention is impaired in paranoid patients. However, most other research workers have reached the opposite conclusion. Weckowicz found that it was the non-paranoid, usually hebephrenic patients who demonstrated the greatest reduction in both size and distance constancy (Weckowicz, 1957; Weckowicz, Somner and Hall, 1958). Patients with predominantly paranoid symptoms were sharply distinguished by showing either visual constancy or *over-estimation* of size and distance. In the later studies by Weckowicz and Blewett (1959) showing a positive correlation between perceptual anomalies and poor conceptual thinking, both these impairments were found to be most evident in the hebephrenic, non-paranoid patient. Similar results have been found by Raush (1952) in his investigations of size estimation in paranoid and non-paranoid groups. In Shakow's (1963) review of his own experimental studies he makes the following comments regarding the differences between the paranoid and hebephrenic sub-groups:

> In 58 measurements which we made on groups of normal, paranoid and hebephrenic subjects, we found the paranoid to be nearer the normal in 31 instances and the hebephrenic nearer the normal in only seven instances. In 20 instances in six quite varied experiments, however, the paranoid and hebephrenic subjects' scores fell on either side of the normals. Thus, these two groups seem consistently to deal with situa-

tions in distinctive ways, giving quite different 'styles' of response (Shakow, 1963).

In the distraction studies reported by McGhie and his colleagues it was found that all positive findings were consistently related to schizophrenic patients who displayed a recognizable pattern of hebephrenic symptoms. Those patients who were markedly distracted in certain aspects of psychomotor performance, on tasks demanding perception and short-term retention and on tests of speech comprehension had all been diagnosed within the hebephrenic sub-type. In striking contrast, those patients with a predominantly paranoid picture had no difficulty in fixing attention on one of a number of competing stimuli. Indeed, on most tests the paranoid group were found to be *less* distractible than the normal control subjects. In most cases the distributions of schizophrenic scores on the tests used were bimodal indicating the presence of two clearly differentiated sub-groups. The high variance of the distributions of the total schizophrenic group scores was accounted for mainly by the blending of paranoid and hebephrenic patients. When these two groups were differentiated and their distractibility scores treated separately, the distributions were now found to be indicative of two homogeneous populations. In another stage of these investigations (Lawson, 1965) all schizophrenic patients who had served as subjects in the distraction experiments were rated on the Wittenborn Psychiatric Rating Scale. When these ratings were examined a significantly *negative* bi-serial correlation was found between paranoid symptomatology and experimentally measured distractibility.

A clear distinction between paranoid and non-paranoid patients is a central feature of Silverman's cognitive control studies. In surveying the findings of others (Silverman, 1964a) and interpreting his own findings (Silverman, 1964b) he concluded that excessive scanning and high field articulation responsiveness are typical of paranoid schizophrenic patients. In contrast to this the performance of non-paranoid schizophrenics is characterized by minimal scanning and poor, undifferentiated, field articulation responsiveness. Although Silverman's results give a picture of the paranoid patient as hyper-alert and excessively scanning his environment, this is not taken to mean that he is cortically 'overloaded'. Silverman employs Bruner's (1957) concept of 'cognitive filtering' to suggest that the sensory input of the paranoid patient is excessively scanned only to facilitate the rejection of input likely to be disturbing to the patient. This process of 'ideational gating' ensures that only stimuli which are acceptable to the paranoid patient's thinking are allowed to enter consciousness at a cortical level:

> Things and events either fit the paranoid schizophrenic's delusional system or they do not exist. Under these conditions, a state of information overload – a state which appears to characterize certain other schizophrenias – is not possible. For there are only two kinds of information to be processed – that which is congruent with one's delusional system and that which is not (Silverman, 1964b).

Silverman's conclusions are thus to some extent congruent with those reached by others in their differentiation of the paranoid and non-paranoid groups.

Some of the investigations of arousal level in schizophrenia have shown differences between paranoid and non-paranoid patients. Venables and Wing (1962) found non-paranoid patients to have a higher fusion threshold for paired light flashes, indicating a state of over arousal. The association between two-flash threshold and skin potential in paranoid patients was similar to that found in normal subjects and the opposite to the antagonistic association found in non-paranoid patients (Venables, 1963). In his use of the S.A.E., Claridge (1967) found paranoid patients to have a lower after-effect than non-paranoid patients, again indicating a lower level of arousal in the former group.

The consensus of opinion of studies directly comparing

paranoid and non-paranoid forms of schizophrenia would appear to be that it is the latter non-paranoid group who shows the most profound breakdown in the selective and inhibitory functions of attention. This is particularly evident in non-paranoid patients of the hebephrenic variety. In contrast to this, paranoid patients show either no attentional dysfunction or a narrowing of the field of attention. There is some suggestion that the more inhibited attentional behaviour of the paranoid patient is one aspect of a defensive strategy against disturbing input.

It is more difficult to make a clear distinction between the arousal level of paranoid and non-paranoid schizophrenics. Although the studies of Venables and Claridge referred to above support the notion that paranoids are under-aroused in comparison with non-paranoid patients, this conclusion is less justified if we include measures of autonomic arousal. Claridge (1967) has reviewed his own and other related findings which suggest that paranoid patients are *over*-aroused on measures of autonomic arousal such as the sedation threshold. These conflicting findings may be accommodated in Claridge's (1967) dual arousal model of the tonic arousal and arousal modulating systems. The paranoid patient would then be seen to be characterized by weak arousal modulation and high tonic arousal, this leading to inhibited and narrowed attention. The non-paranoid (mainly hebephrenic) patient would be distinguished by a low level of tonic arousal but an over-functioning modulating system causing a lack of control over incoming stimulation.

The acute and chronic comparison

The fact that the majority of studies of schizophrenia have employed chronic patients probably reflects the greater unreliability of diagnosis in the earlier acute stage. Although Shakow's studies have been confined mainly to chronic patients, his observations of a small number of acute patients convinced him that there was surprisingly little difference in the attentional performance of the two groups. However, he did observe a difference in the emotional reaction of the acute patient to his increased awareness of peripheral features in the stimulus field. Shakow suggested that acute patients are at first excited by this wider area of experience and react to it with the same fascinated delight as L.S.D. subjects react to a somewhat similar experience. The chronic patient, who has become more adapted to such changes in his attention, shows no particular affective reaction. McGhie and his colleagues found no significant differences in the distractibility of their acute and chronic patients although, like Shakow, they did note a difference in their affective reactions.

Although most investigations of perceptual constancy have been restricted to more chronic groups of patients there is some suggestion that reduced size and distance constancy is less frequent in acute schizophrenic patients. One study (Lovinger, 1956) found that patients rated as being in good contact with their environment showed as good perceptual constancy as normal controls, whereas poor contact patients showed a reduction in constancy. As Lovinger's poor contact patients were mainly chronic and his good contact patients mainly at the acute stage of their illness this might be taken as further confirmation that selective attention is less disturbed in the early stage of the illness. Some of Silverman's (1964b) work suggests that the extensive field scanning shown by paranoid patients lessens as the patients become more chronic. Silverman has also made the suggestion that some of the differences in attentional behaviour of acute and chronic patients may be a consequence of the chronic patients adopting certain strategies which enable them to deal more effectively with an environment which threatens to overload and engulf them. A similar point has been made by McGhie and his colleagues who noted that their chronic patients often resorted to activities, such as plugging their ears and sitting with their eyes closed, to reduce the amount of environmental stimulation and aid their concentration.

Most studies of arousal in which comparisons have been made between acute and chronic patients indicate a higher level of arousal in the chronic group. We have already made reference to a number of studies which have shown higher sedation thresholds for chronic than acute patients. Some workers have produced further evidence of such arousal differences by assessing the effects of depressant drugs on the level of attention and general clinical state of schizophrenic patients. This approach has indicated that chronic patients improve and show a nearer normal level of attention under such drugs which are known to lower arousal levels (Fulcher, Gallagher and Pfeiffer, 1957). Work reported by Williams (1953), Malmo, Shagass and David (1951), and Venables and Wing (1962) adds further support to the view that autonomic arousal is higher in chronic patients.

The relative lack of information on changes in attentional behaviour occurring during the acute phase of a schizophrenic illness makes it difficult to come to any clear conclusions regarding acute/chronic differences. Measures of arousal suggest that the basic level of activation changes during the progress of the illness. Most psychological measurements of attentional dysfunction demonstrate a widening of attention in all schizophrenics except paranoid patients. It is possible that any differences which do exist might reflect various behavioural strategies adopted by the chronic patient to reduce the flow of stimulation to a more tolerable level. Another source of difficulty in making comparisons of the acute and chronic patient lies in the simple fact that chronic patients are more likely to show behavioural changes induced by long periods in institutions. Such changes are notoriously difficult to distinguish from changes which might be an inherent part of the disease process. Apart from the differences in the social environment of the two groups, chronic patients are exposed to a different diet, different pharmacological régimes and different therapeutic attitudes from acutely ill patients. They are likely to be considerably older than acute patients so that the ageing process may itself act as an uncontrolled variable. The general motivation of the more recently ill, acute patient is likely to be considerably higher than his chronic counterpart who may value less the reinforcement of pleasing the investigator by cooperating well. Indeed, in a modern research and teaching hospital the chronic patient may be rendered 'test-sophisticated' and blasé by repeated investigations at the hands of a changing parade of enthusiastic research workers. All such factors may easily interact to confuse the picture of acute/chronic differences. The overlapping between the acute/chronic dichotomy with other sub-classifications of schizophrenia is likely to confuse the picture even more. There is a clear need for prospective longitudinal studies to examine changes in attentional behaviour of patients from the early acute stages of their illness through to the more chronic phase.

Process and reactive comparisons

Studies of attentional performance of process and reactive schizophrenics are few and the results of those which have been reported tend to be obscured by the vagueness and ambiguity of the two categories. Harris (1957) studied the size estimation of patients graded on the basis of a prognostic scale as process and reactive. He found that the process schizophrenics tended to be characterized by minimal scanning behaviour while the reactive schizophrenics were characterized by extensive scanning behaviour. Bryant (1961) found similar results using an embedded figures test and Witkin's rod and frame test.

Claridge (1967) reviews two unpublished studies of process-reactive comparisons on the S.A.E. and sedation threshold tests. In the first study (carried out by Hume and Treacher) a group of schizophrenic patients were classified as process or reactive according to their ratings on the premorbid history section of the Phillip's Prognostic Scale (1953). No differences emerged between the two groups on either sedation threshold or S.A.E. Although similar negative results were again evident using a different method of clinical assessment, there was a slight but non-significant increase in S.A.E. with worsening prognosis. In another study by Wawman, process schizophrenic patients were found to have lower sedation thresholds and longer S.A.E.s than reactive patients. In his own work Claridge (1967) found that reactive patients performed much better than process patients on the auditory vigilance task described earlier in this chapter.

The methods used for categorizing patients within the process-reactive scheme are such that there is bound to be a great deal of overlap between the process group and the hebephrenic category. Indeed, McGhie and his colleagues (1965) found that when they used a specially designed rating scale to differentiate process schizophrenics from a mixed group of patients, almost all of those rated as process patients had been previously diagnosed as hebephrenic by the psychiatrists in charge of their case. Some psychiatrists have commented upon the resemblance between the nuclear, hebephrenic, or process form of schizophrenia and various types of organic dementia. With this in mind Lawson, McGhie and Chapman (1967) repeated some of their previous distraction studies with matched groups of schizophrenic patients, non-schizophrenic psychotic patients, normal controls *and* with a group of patients having a diagnosis of arteriosclerotic dementia. This study replicated their previous findings but also indicated a clear similarity in performance between hebephrenic and arteriosclerotic patients. Similar results have been arrived at by a few other workers who have compared schizophrenic and brain-damaged patients. Weckowicz (1960), using the Gottschaldt Hidden Pictures Test, found that schizophrenic patients were significantly more distracted by the irrelevant background than other groups of psychotic patients, but that their performance did not differ from that of brain-damaged patients. Feinberg and Mercer (1960) used Chapman's (1956) test of distractibility and associative intrusion to find a similar parallel between the more malignant type of schizophrenic illness and organic cerebral disease.

Summary of Intra-Group Studies

If we can regard schizophrenia as a gigantic jigsaw, the study of its intra-group differences would appear to be a first essential step which allows us to put some of the pieces together in a meaningful way. However, many of the pieces are still missing and a great deal more research is obviously necessary before a clear picture emerges of the attentional dysfunction which appears to be a prominent feature of at least some varieties of schizophrenia. Shakow (1962) has given a rather picturesque but accurate summary of the various sub-group differences in a vivid analogy of a person walking through a wood:

> If he is of the paranoid persuasion he sticks even more closely than the normal person to the path through the forest, examining each tree along the path, and sometimes even each tree's leaves, with meticulous care ... if at the other extreme, he follows the hebephrenic pattern then he acts as though there were no paths for he strays off the obvious ones entirely, ... he is attracted ... by any and all trees, and even the undergrowth and floor of the forest in a superficial, flitting way, apparently forgetting in the meantime about the place he wants to get to ... my impression is that the acute patient in the same forest undergoes a multitude of fairly new experiences reacting highly affectively, for instance, to new and unusual patterns of light on the leaves, or to novel and subtle patterns of form in the branches.

There is clear experimental support for those clinicians who would mark off the paranoid group from that of all other forms of schizophrenia. Patients with a predominantly paranoid symptomatology demonstrate a highly selective type of attention which enables them to screen out extraneous stimulation more efficiently than normal subjects. It is possible that the suggestion made by such workers as Silverman is correct, and that the filter mechanism of the paranoid patient is set to attend selectively only to events which might interfere with the rationale of his delusional system. Some years ago Cameron (1951) described how the paranoid patient restricts himself 'to watching with his newly acquired reaction sensitivity and making selections which confirm his favoured hypotheses ... the patient excludes whatever he cannot handle regardless of its importance ... everything that can be made congruent gets absorbed into the vectors of the developing (delusional) system, even although this system may not correspond with the social fact.' However, this distinction is blurred by the ambiguous nature of the criteria used for diagnosing the paranoid group. Many schizophrenics entertain transient delusions during the course of their illness although these may be embedded in a welter of other schizophrenic symptoms. In other patients, a highly elaborated system of delusional thinking is a prominent feature of the illness and may exist in the absence of other schizophrenic symptoms. Some clinicians would feel that the inclusion of such paranoid patients within the schizophrenic group merely obscures the clinical picture, and that they should be regarded as constituting an entirely separate psychotic group. The findings of most studies of disturbed attention in schizophrenic patients would support such a conclusion.

Consistent findings have also been reported in respect of another sub-group of schizophrenia which stands in vivid contrast to the paranoid group. It is probably of little importance whether we label this sub-group 'hebephrenic', 'nuclear' or 'process'. The patients in this category show an insidious onset to their illness, marked thought disorder, loss of affect and a tendency to progress to a chronic deteriorating state. The clinical picture is almost identical with the original Kraepelinian description of dementia praecox. The experimental work with this group suggests that the normal processes of selection and inhibition governing attention have broken down so that the patients suffer from a marked inability to select stimuli in such a way that only relevant information is processed. The effect of this impairment of selective attention on the performance of the schizophrenic patients will vary with a number of factors including the amount of information to be processed in any situation, the particular modality in which the information is presented, and the rate of arrival of information. There is some suggestion that the breakdown in selective attention exhibited by these patients is the result of a state of over-arousal of the reticular activating system, or of a failure in the normal homeostatic control between sub-cortical and cortical centres. There is also some suggestion that this group of patients may have an underlying organic pathology. The issue regarding changes in attention between the acute and chronic phases of the illness is still somewhat obscure. There is some evidence that during the acute phase, selective attention is less impaired and that such impairment as there is is variable so that the patient's behaviour may fluctuate widely from one time to another. There is an obvious need for more systematic studies which not only attempt to clearly separate the different sub-groups of the illness during the acute stage but also to identify, by repeated examination, at what stage of the illness the disorder of attentive behaviour becomes apparent.

After we have dealt with the paranoid and nuclear groups we are still left with a variety of patients who are diagnosed as suffering from schizophrenia but who do not fit in to either of these two sub-categories. It is possible that subsequent work will help to define, in more precise terms, the condition of such patients and they may well be eventually reallocated to other diagnostic groups outside that of schizophrenia.

Conclusion

One great disadvantage in a book of this nature is that one is limited to considering only one aspect of human behaviour, in this case that of attention. This limitation is perhaps nowhere more evident than when we attempt to consider such a complex psychopathological problem as schizophrenia. Studies of changes in other cognitive processes such as learning, memory, and thinking, and in non-cognitive areas such as motivation and interpersonal relationships, to be considered in later volumes in this series, add much to our understanding of the bizarre and highly complex behaviour of the schizophrenic patient. In an illness involving such severe disorganization of personality it would be surprising to find that only one mental process was implicated. However, there seems little doubt that the mechanisms responsible for the direction and control of attention are disrupted in many schizophrenic patients. This disturbance may manifest itself in heightened distractibility, failure to hold and pursue required mental sets, abnormal levels of arousal or in other directions considered in this review. As attention is the first essential stage in coming to terms with the environment it seems likely that a disturbance at this level will have a reverberating effect on all other mental functions involved at later stages of the learning process. To this extent, the attentional deficit may be regarded as a basic part of schizophrenic psychopathology, although its underlying cause remains obscure.

An understanding of the patient's attentional difficulties allows us to speculate upon the ideal type of environment for the schizophrenic patient in hospital. Chapman and McGhie (1963) have observed that secondary symptoms such as hallucinations, catatonic behaviour and social withdrawal are likely to be intensified where the patient finds himself in large noisy wards where his senses are constantly bombarded by multiple stimuli. These workers have also put forward some simple practical suggestions aimed at facilitating communication with the individual schizophrenic patient. They have suggested, for example, that verbal communication may be greatly improved if the patient is presented with small, well-structured verbal units and extraneous sources of stimulation are minimized.

5 Organic Brain Damage

The Clinical Picture

The broad diagnostic category of patients with organic brain damage includes all those whose psychiatric symptoms are a result of known disease or injury to the brain and central nervous system. It is clear that the symptoms and behaviour changes exhibited by brain-damaged patients will vary considerably depending on such factors as the extent and severity of brain pathology, the locus of the damage within the brain and with the personality of the individual patient. However, clinical studies suggest that certain patterns of symptoms are so commonly found in brain-damaged patients as to permit us to refer to the '*brain-damage syndrome*'. The symptoms which constitute this syndrome have been described as follows:

1. ... impairment of comprehension, interference with elaboration of impressions, defects in orientation and retention, difficulty in activation of memories and *marked fluctuation of the level of attention.*
2. Affective disorder in the forms of emotional stability ...
3. Character change in the form of conduct foreign to the patient's natural disposition ... (Henderson and Gillespie, 1962).

The category of organic brain damage is often divided into the two sub-categories of *acute* and *chronic* brain damage. The acute group normally includes patients whose symptoms are a result of the temporary action of a toxic process affecting the normal functioning of the brain (e.g. febrile illness, the action of alcohol or other noxious drugs). Within the chronic category are grouped patients whose disturbed condition is a result of a more permanent, and usually more severe, damage to the structure of the brain. The vast majority of psychological investigations have been concerned with this latter category of chronic brain damage. The chronic category may itself be usefully sub-divided into conditions involving diffuse damage throughout the brain and those where the damage is more specific and localized in one region of the brain.

Perhaps the most common categories of diffuse generalized brain damage are those disease processes associated with senescence and senility. Patients in this category constitute a rapidly increasing problem for the psychiatric and geriatric services. In 1900 the proportion of people in Great Britain over pensionable age was one in seventeen. In 1961 this proportion had increased to one in six and is still increasing today. The rapid expansion of elderly people in the community at risk to the organic dementias of later life has led to a doubling of the number of elderly people admitted to mental hospitals over the last half century. In a survey carried out in one English region (Kay, Beemish and Roth, 1964) it was found that one in ten of the over sixty-five-year-old population appeared to be suffering from an organic brain syndrome. In about half of these cases the degree of dementia was similar in form and severity to that found in demented hospital patients.

Some forms of organic dementia have their onset somewhat before senescence and are grouped together under the general heading of *presenile psychotic illnesses*. The main symptoms of such conditions are deterioration in reasoning and judgement, impairment of recent memory, and an increasing impairment of socialized, goal-directed behaviour. *Senile psychoses*, with its onset after the age of sixty years, constitute a much larger diagnostic group and is associated with a general shrinking of the brain and wastage of the brain's nerve cells. The onset of symptoms may be gradual but usually includes memory deficit, poor orientation for time and space, intellectual deterioration, episodes of confused uncontrolled behaviour and deterioration in personal habits. There is some disagreement as to whether the distinction between the changes occurring in senile dementia and normal ageing is a qualitative or quantitative one. Certainly the resemblance of the clinical picture of dementia to that of the normal ageing process ensures that the wealth of information yielded by studies of age changes is highly relevant to our understanding of senile dementia. Indeed, the factors which finally decide whether some elderly people are admitted to a mental hospital or remain within the community are often purely social, reflecting the tolerance of relatives, friends and neighbours. An elderly neighbour of the present author remained at home for over eight years although obviously very seriously demented. Finally, in one of her many confused states, she one day ran along the street naked. The following day she was admitted to the local mental hospital.

The remaining group of brain-damaged patients are those whose psychiatric symptoms are a consequence of specific and localized damage to brain tissue either through external foci (head injury) or internal foci (circumscribed tumours). It is perhaps worth emphasizing here that the psychiatrist and clinical psychologist are not normally concerned with all such neurological patients, but only those whose brain damage precipitates or accompanies neurotic or psychotic symptoms. It might be added that the patient's symptoms may reflect not only the location and severity of his brain damage but also the reaction of his personality to the brain injury. With such localized lesions the site of the damage may greatly influence the behavioural changes displayed by the patient. While psychological and neurological studies have amassed much information on the functions of different regions of the brain and the behavioural dysfunctions caused by their destruction or impairment, the picture is still too ambiguous to establish anything approaching a one-to-one relationship between location of the lesion and subsequent behavioural changes.

The contribution of psychological research to the assessment of the effects of brain damage has been disappointingly limited. The prolonged concentration on the assessment of intellectual deterioration as a psychological synonym for brain damage has done little to advance our knowledge of the effects of brain damage on behaviour. The standard tests of intellectual deterioration yield measurements which are too crude to be of any real diagnostic significance, although they may provide a useful base-line measure for subsequent assessments of the progress of an organic dementia. Full and detailed criticism of such blanket approaches to the psychometric assessment of organic brain deficit have been adequately reported elsewhere (e.g. Meyer, 1961; Piercy, 1964) and need not be repeated here. In more recent years there has been a healthy tendency for psychologists to forsake this approach and to concentrate their skills in developing techniques designed to provide more specific information on the changes in different mental functions concomitant with brain damage. A considerable amount of information has been accumulated on the effect of different types of brain lesions upon the normal memory process. The effects of diffuse brain disease are perhaps more difficult to investigate but there are increasing indications that the information derived from experimental studies of normal ageing is being utilized in the study of senile states. Unfortunately, the expertise and technical resources of many psychologists is undermined by their comparative ignorance of neurological and clinical matters. Similarly many psychiatrists and neurologists are restricted in their investigations by their unfamiliarity with the techniques and findings of the psychological approach to the assessment of behavioural changes. There is a strong argument in favour of more joint work based upon a team approach to the study of brain damage with each participant able to contribute a vital piece of the jig-saw.

The process of attention and its relation to brain pathology has been rather sparsely studied in comparison with many other mental functions such as learning and memory. In this chapter we will consider the findings of some of the studies of attentional dysfunction in brain-damaged patients and their clinical significance.

Experimental Studies of Brain-Damaged Populations

Distractibility

Perhaps the most common form of attentional deficit to be associated with brain-damaged patients is a failure in the normal inhibitory processes resulting in abnormal distractibility. Kraepelin used the term 'hyperosexia' to denote a state of exaggerated arousal of attention in which the patient found difficulty in ignoring any stimuli in his immediate environment. In his careful studies of brain-damaged adults Goldstein (1939) suggested that one of the most characteristic features of the brain-damage syndrome was a 'forced responsiveness' to stimuli. Goldstein observed that the apparent inattentiveness of such patients was a consequence of their involuntary attentiveness to inessential elements of the stimulus situation. Thus their attempts to attend to the 'interviewer's' questions were constantly frustrated by their forced responsiveness to external noises, the texture of the interviewer's clothing, the speaker's gestures, or to any other stimuli which would be normally ignored. Goldstein was particularly interested in that aspect of distractibility demonstrated by the patient's inability to make a clear perceptual distinction between figure and ground. He described many situations where the patient's perception and concentration was disrupted by the intrusion of background elements. A difficulty in isolating a visual figure from a distracting background had been investigated earlier by Poppelreuter (1918) who maintained that this type of failure in visual discrimination was due to specific injury to the central visual pathways, rather than representing a general feature of brain damage. Goldstein

(1927) disagreed with the specificity of the 'figure-ground' syndrome as a visual-motor effect, seeing it as one example of a general loss of discrimination found in all brain-damaged patients.

Goldstein's 'figure-ground' syndrome was later investigated in much more detail by Werner and Strauss in a series of studies of brain-damaged children. These workers used a test involving the reproduction of patterns on a board containing ten rows of ten holes. The pattern is constructed by filling in some of the holes with coloured marbles and the child is asked first to copy the pattern and then subsequently to reproduce it in a line drawing (see Figure 13).

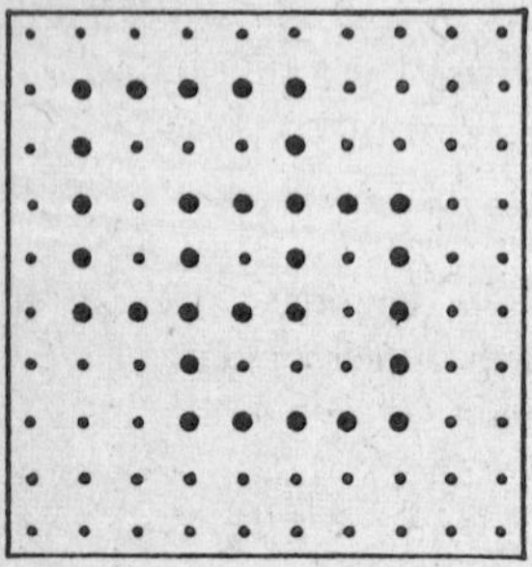

Figure 13 Example of marble board patterns in Werner and Strauss's (1939) study

Normal and non-brain-injured defective children tended to adopt a planned and continuous approach to constructing the pattern whereas the brain-damaged child's performance was characteristically sporadic and discontinuous (see Figure 14).

The poor performance of the brain-damaged children on this task was interpreted by Werner and Strauss (1939) as being due to the distracting effect of the background holes. To examine this further they constructed a modified version of the test where the background was intentionally

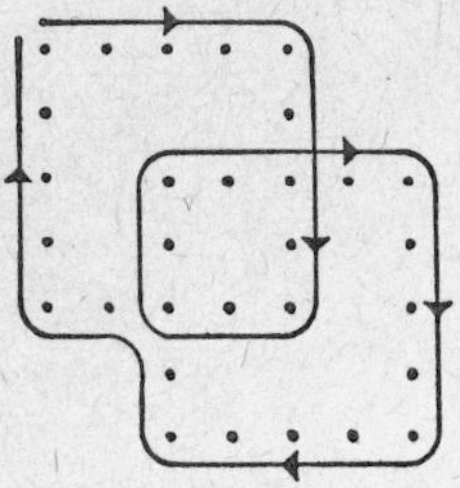

non-brain-damaged

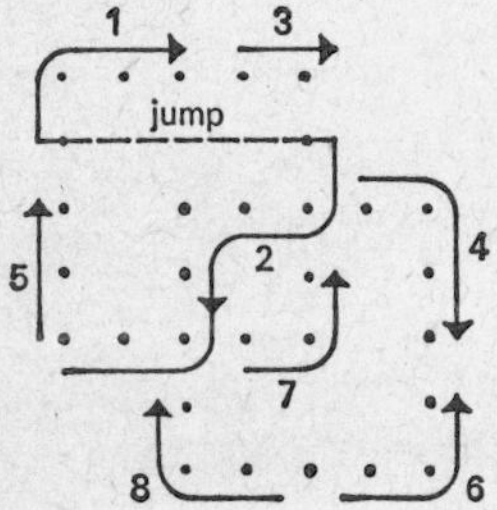

brain-damaged

Figure 14 Example of the performance of normal and brain-damaged children (Werner and Strauss, 1939)

structured to be at variance with the patterns formed by the marbles.

The performance of brain-damaged children on this test showed clear evidence of the effect of background attraction on performance (Werner and Strauss, 1941). Although normal children were also distracted by the background patterns, their reproductions, even when incorrect, reflected an organized figure. In contrast, the inability of brain-damaged children to inhibit the influence of the distracting background resulted in a totally disorganized figure (see Figure 15).

Similar findings were observed when subjects were presented with brief tachistoscopic exposures of simple

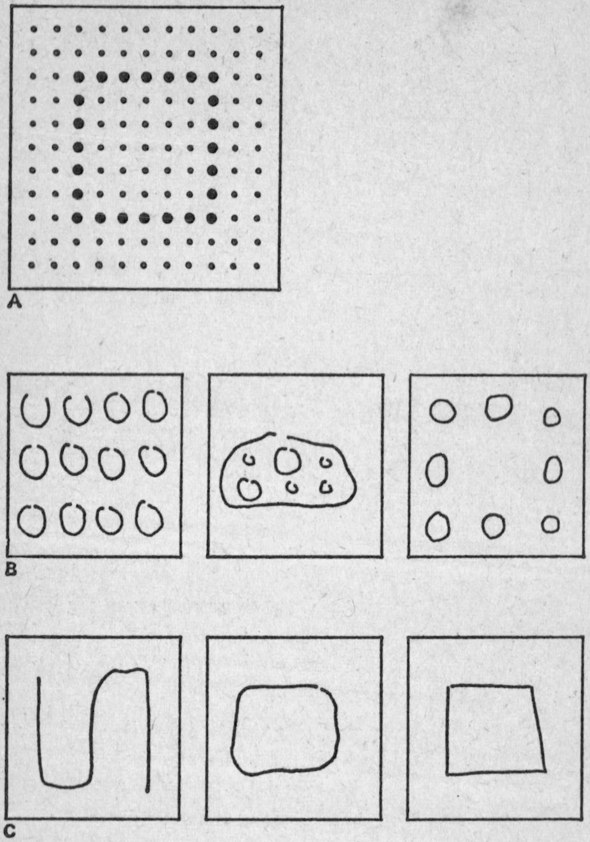

Figure 15 Tactual-motor test pattern. A: model. B: copies by brain-damaged children. C: copies by endogenous children

figures embedded in distracting line backgrounds (Werner and Strauss, 1941) (see Figure 16).

Although normal children again found the background distracting and gave some responses contaminated by the background, proportion of such figure-background confusion responses given by the normal children was small (9

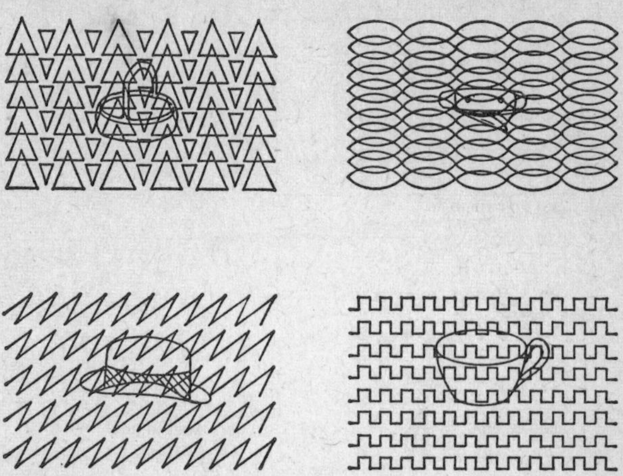

Figure 16 Example of embedded figures in Werner and Strauss's (1941) study

per cent) in comparison with the brain-damaged children (75 per cent). Werner and Strauss later extended their studies to other sensory modalities in order to support their view that this type of attentional impairment was not restricted to the visuo-motor field, but rather constituted a general factor in organic impairment. A tactile equivalent of the marble-board test was used to examine the intrusion of background elements on tactile performance. Here the child's task was to explore tactually patterns constructed by raised rubber tacks while ignoring the background interference of flat enamelled thumb tacks. Again it was found (Werner and Strauss, 1941) that the performance of brain-damaged children was strikingly disrupted by the diffuse background (see Figure 17). Werner and Bowers (1941) found a similar effect on a test of auditory perception and later work illustrated the effect of background stimulation on tests involving memory (Werner, 1946) and concept formation (Werner, 1949).

In a more recent report (Deutsch and Zawel, 1966) it is

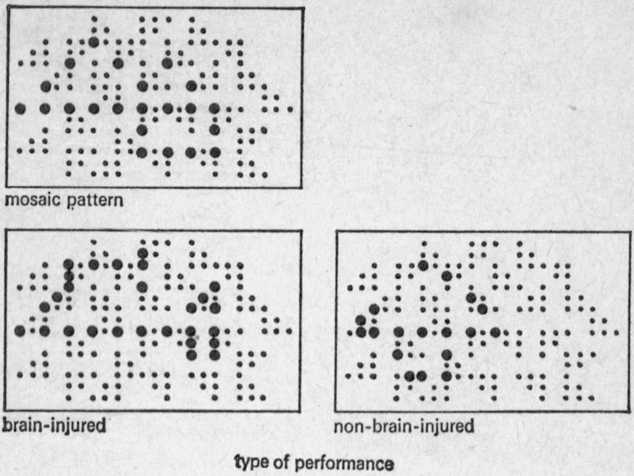

Figure 17 Typical representations of normal and brain-damaged children in tactile tests (Werner and Strauss, 1941)

suggested that, although the background distraction may be intrusive in all aspects of the brain-damaged patient's performance, it is more pronounced in the auditory modality. This investigation employed a series of visual figure-ground differentiation tasks in which the form of the distracting background varied in meaningfulness. In a second (auditory distraction) condition a parallel series of tests of auditory perception were presented in the presence of different levels of auditory distraction again varying in meaningfulness (from white noise to actual recordings of conversations). Analysis of the data showed that, while the performance of normal children varied with the difficulty of the task regardless of modality, that of brain-damaged children was inclined to be modality specific. In this situation it was the auditory distracting condition which affected the perceptual performance of the brain-damaged children. Lawson, McGhie and Chapman (1961) reported a similar modality-specific effect using tests of distraction with brain-damaged, arteriosclerotic, adult patients. Although this latter study again demonstrated a greater distraction effect on auditory perceptual tasks it was also observed that the visual perceptual performance of the brain-damaged patients was so poor *without* distraction that the effects of distraction on this modality may have been masked. As Deutsch and Zawel (1966) did not present data on basic scores on their tests without distraction it is not possible to assess whether a similar explanation may apply to their findings.

The interpretation that such findings may be regarded as a breakdown in selective perception has been challenged by Spivack (1963) who has criticized the methodology of figure-background experiments. Spivack points out that what is termed the 'background' is often the dominant feature of the presentation in so far as it occupies more of the stimulus space than the 'figure'. As the subject is normally asked to report what he sees, the fact that he reports the background may merely reflect the patient's indecision regarding the correct test strategy. A similar objection may be levelled at the system of scoring in figure-background experiments in other modalities. In surveying this work Spivack concludes that 'the question remains open about whether such performance reflects a basic defect in brain-injured subjects in the capacity to disregard background, or the tendency for dominant aspects of complex stimuli to intrude upon or dampen less dominant features, or whether the research techniques have allowed non-perceptual response characteristics to guide performance' (Spivack, 1963). Another possible criticism that figure-background impairment is a phenomenon restricted mainly to brain-damaged patients with specific sensory defects would appear to be answered by investigations reported by Yacorzynsky and Davis (1945) and Teuber and Weinstein (1956). Both these studies failed to find any explicit association between figure-background impairment and visual field defect. Teuber and Weinstein found that a group of brain-injured servicemen performed the Gottschaldt Embedded Figures Test at a significantly lower level than a matched group of non-brain-damaged controls. However, test performance was found to be unrelated to the presence or absence of visual field defects. Teuber and Weinstein did note that those brain-damaged patients who were known to be aphasic tended to have more difficulty in this test than non-aphasic, brain-damaged patients.

A more recent study by Russo and Vignolo (1967) has attempted to examine in a more systematic manner this suggested association between figure-background impairment and aphasia. Their experimental group was composed of ninety-five patients with *unilateral*, hemispheric lesions who had been assessed on tests for visual field defects and aphasia. The Gottschaldt Embedded Figure Test was given to all subjects according to a standard procedure and scoring system devised by Thurstone (1944) in his use of the test with normal subjects. This procedure obviates many of the objections raised by Spivack in that the subject is left in no doubt as to the figure which he is required to discriminate. However, Spivack's other criticism, that the embedding background is a dominant part of the stimulus, would still apply to this procedure. The findings of this experiment confirm Teuber and Weinstein's finding that poor figure-background differentiation is associated with brain damage but more prominently with aphasia. The findings are, however, complicated by the fact that the performance of non-aphasic patients varied greatly with the hemispherical location of the brain damage. Non-aphasic patients with right hemispherical damage performed almost as well as normal controls. The most obvious explanation that patients with right hemispherical lesions were more severely brain-damaged than non-aphasic patients with left hemispherical lesions was rejected by Russo and Vignolo on rather tenuous grounds. Their main criteria for assessing the degree of brain damage was based upon the scores obtained on a visual reaction time test. This rather unusual method of assessing the severity of brain damage was based on an earlier study (De Renzi and Faglioni, 1965) which showed a small positive correlation with the degree of cerebral involvement. Russo and Vignolo's own interpretation of their findings is that poor visual figure-background discrimination results from a defect in visual-spatial orientation associated with damage to the right hemisphere of the brain. This interpretation is in line with other reports (e.g. Milner, 1958) that hemispherical damage results in an impairment in the perception and short-term storage of visual, non-verbal information. It does not, however, explain the additional finding that aphasic (left hemispherical damage) patients also show a pronounced figure-background impairment.

A recent study of brain-damaged children by Schulman, Kasper and Throne (1965) has observed a close association between brain damage and several measures of distractibility. These workers set out to examine the four symptoms of hyperactivity, inconsistency, emotional liability and distractibility, which have been associated with brain damage so frequently that they have been taken to be the main constituents of the 'brain-damage syndrome'. To this purpose they employed a battery of tests and experimental techniques designed to measure the presence and degree of each of these four symptoms. The absence of any significant correlations between the test measurements of the four symptoms led Schulman and his colleagues to conclude that their combination as a distinct syndrome was not justified. The one positive finding which did emerge from their investigations was that the measures of distractibility not only intercorrelated with each other but together provided a usefully reliable indication of the presence and degree of brain damage. In their final conclusions, Schulman and his co-workers state, 'the only variable which approached unequivocal support as a correlate of brain damage, regardless of extent or location of damage, was distractibility . . . the capacity to maintain attention may be a consequence of cortical integration of neural impulses which may be disrupted by damage' (Schulman, Kasper and Throne, 1965). Unfortunately the significance of these findings is somewhat obscured by the rather ambiguous criterion of brain damage adopted in selection of subjects. Selection was based on the assumption that children below a certain I.Q. level were more likely to be brain-damaged than children above that level, so that the I.Q. acted as a criterion score in the diagnosis of brain damage.

'Distractibility' is itself a very complex factor and much depends upon the techniques used in measuring its effects. In many studies the distracting stimuli are themselves meaningful and may even require a secondary response from the subject. High distraction scores may then reflect the subject's inability to act in accordance with the experimenter's own distinction between relevant and irrelevant aspects of the stimulus presentation, rather than failure to inhibit known irrelevancies. Such difficulties in interpretation are extensions of the criticisms levelled by Spivack on the figure-background discrimination studies.

In studies where the irrelevant distracting stimuli are clearly defined and made meaningless in comparison to the meaningful relevant stimuli, differences between brain-damaged and normal adult populations are less distinct. Schlanger (1958) assessed the effect of auditory background noise on the auditory discrimination of brain-damaged patients. Subjects were required to discriminate between similar sounding words (e.g. pin and pen) and then to select the picture of the objects named from a number of alternatives. Schlanger found that the interference effect of the distracting background noise was no greater with brain-damaged patients than non-brain-damaged controls.

Distribution of attention

In tasks where the secondary distracting stimulus is both meaningful and requires a definite response from the subject, a poor performance may represent an inability to switch attention between two competing stimuli presented simultaneously or in temporal proximity. Birch and his colleagues have developed a rather ingenious technique to assess the effect of brain damage on the ability to attend and respond to two successively presented stimuli. Their original method (Birch, Belmont and Karp, 1964) required the patient to indicate which of two successively presented and objectively identical, auditory stimuli seemed louder to him. The time interval between the pairs of stimuli was varied to allow these workers to study the temporal effects of antecedent stimulation upon the individual's responsiveness to a subsequent stimulus. When normal, non-brain-damaged subjects were placed in this situation they showed a strong tendency either to judge the stimuli as being equal or to over-estimate the intensity of the second tone which was judged to be the louder of the two. In contrast, brain-damaged patients were found to under-estimate the intensity of the second tone, particularly if the interval between presentation of the two tones was very brief. This inhibitory effect of the first stimulus upon the second decreased progressively as the interval between the two stimuli was lengthened. Birch and his colleagues interpreted these findings to suggest that the latency period of recovery from inhibition is increased by brain damage. In order to test this hypothesis they extrapolated their results from a hypothetical curve representing the predicted course of recovery from inhibition in brain-damaged patients (see Figure 18).

This hypothetical curve allowed them to predict that, at an 8-second interval of separation between the tones, the brain-damaged patients should begin to approach the response of the non-brain-damaged patient by over-estimating the intensity of the second tone. At a 9-second interval the over-estimation of the second tone should be identical to that shown by the control subjects when a 3-second interval separated the two stimuli. These predictions were tested in a further study (Birch, Belmont and Karp, 1965) to show that the performance of brain-damaged patients changed in accordance with their pre-

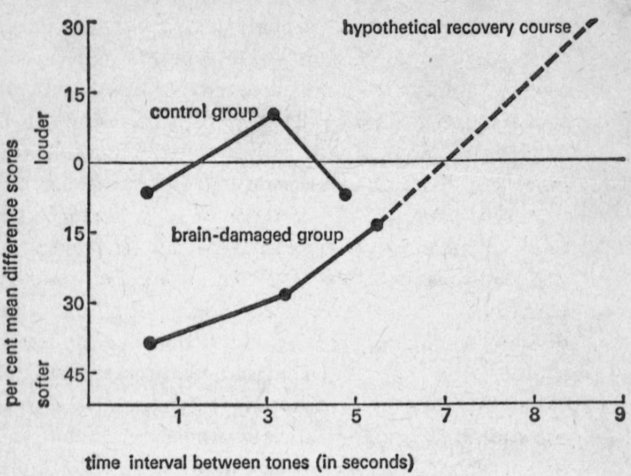

Figure 18 Comparative judgement of the relative intensity of the second of two successfully presented identical tones made by normal and brain-damaged groups (Birch et al., *1964)*

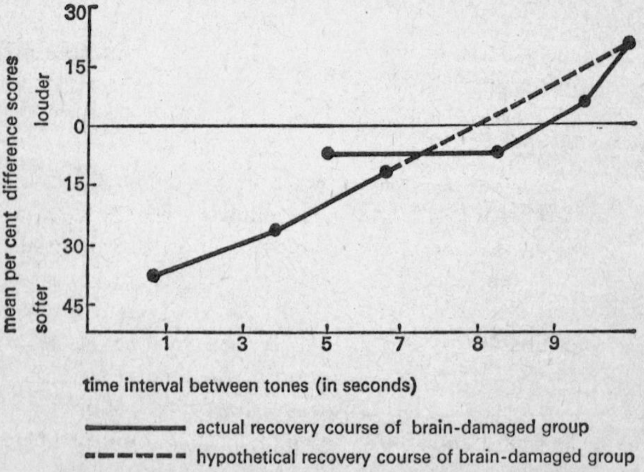

Figure 19 Comparison of actual and hypothetical recovery course shown by brain-damaged group (Birch, et al., *1965)*

dictions to a more 'normal' performance at an interval of nine seconds between the tones (see Figure 19).

In a more recent report (Birch, Belmont and Karp, 1967) a modified form of this procedure was used to investigate patients whose cerebral damage was restricted to one hemisphere. On the basis of their previous work they hypothesized that patients with unilateral damage should demonstrate a slower processing of information of any stimuli being registered in the damaged side of the brain. A secondary related hypothesis led them to expect that stimuli being registered in the non-damaged intact hemisphere would interfere with the processing of information in the damaged hemisphere. In this experiment the stimuli used were electric shocks of low intensity administered to the right and left forearms. Three conditions of stimuli presentation were employed – pairs of simultaneous stimuli; pairs in which the affected side was stimulated in advance of the intact side; pairs of stimuli in which the affected side was stimulated in advance of the intact side. The three specific hypotheses examined by Birch and his co-workers were as follows:

1. When stimulation is bilateral and simultaneous the slower processing of information on the damaged hemisphere should ensure that the intact hemisphere would be processing sensory input in advance of the affected hemisphere.

2. When stimulation is bilateral and successive the first stimulus should be registered in the damaged hemisphere if the time interval between the stimuli is arranged appropriately.

3. When the time interval between two successive stimuli is increased beyond the critical interval necessary for the patient's awareness of the two inputs, the stimulus arriving at the damaged side will have an attentional priority. The registration of the stimulus in the damaged hemisphere will inhibit the later developing activity in the intact side so that the original condition will be reversed. By appropriate timing of the interval the patient will now fail to be aware of the stimulus reaching the intact hemisphere.

The models upon which these inferences are based are represented in Figures 20, 21 and 22.

Each of these predictions was confirmed in subsequent experiments with unilaterally brain-damaged patients. After considering a number of possible explanations of such findings these authors concluded that a slowing down in the physiological processing rate is a common consequence of brain damage. Where the damage is confined to

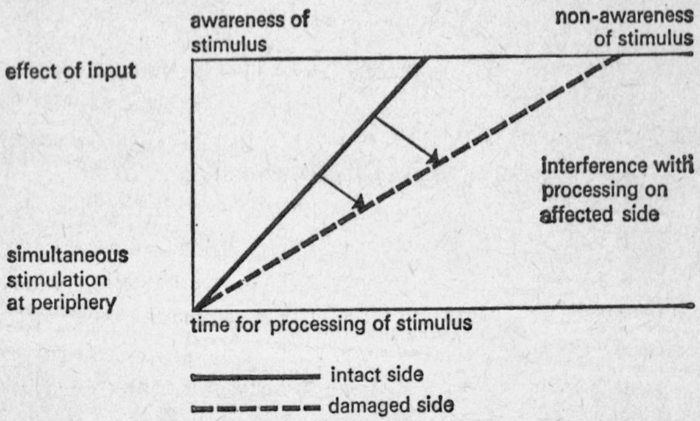

Figure 20 A model for extinction of awareness to double simultaneous homologous stimulation in patients with unilateral cerebral damage (*Birch* et al., *1967*)

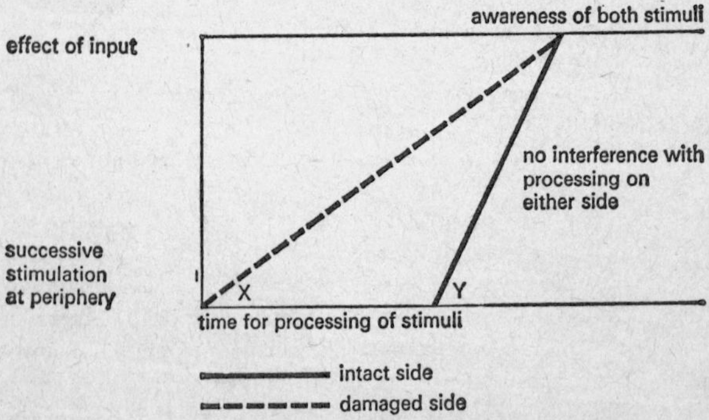

Figure 21 Model for overcoming extinction of awareness to double successive stimulant (*Birch* et al., *1967*)

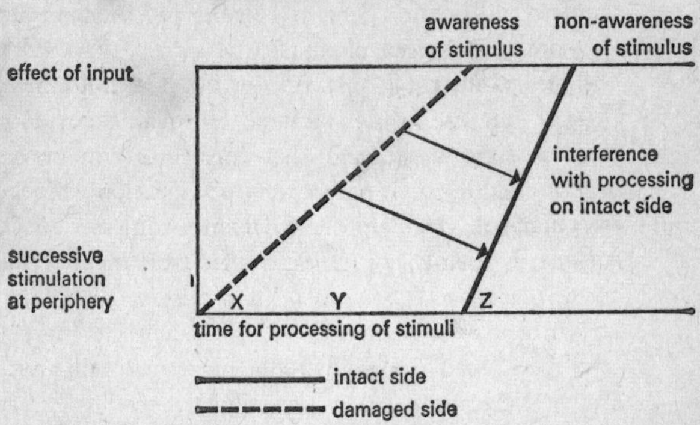

Figure 22 Model of extinction of awareness on the intact side to double successive stimulant (Birch et al., *1967)*

one cerebral hemisphere the reduction in afferent processing will be evident only in the case of information being transmitted to the damaged hemisphere. In their opinion this alteration in processing rate is the basic cause of many of the disturbances of attentive behaviour observed in brain-damaged patients.

Another method of examining the distribution of attention between two stimuli has been developed by Luria and used extensively in his studies of minimally brain-damaged children. The concept of minimal brain damage is relatively new and requires some explanation. This term has been applied to some children who, although of adequate intelligence, show pronounced and consistent learning and behavioural difficulties which are not obviously related to environmental factors. The behavioural symptoms which have been included within the minimal brain-damage syndrome include inattentiveness, impulsiveness, hyperactivity, emotional lability, inability to delay gratification and specific learning impairments. Although the term has been used for some time in Russia and some other countries it has only recently been employed in Western neuro-psychiatry. Stott (1962) has argued that signs of minimal brain damage are frequently found in delinquent children, and child specialists in the U.S.A. have accepted the concept as a useful diagnostic term (Clements, 1966).

Signs of neurological disorder in such children may be present but are equivocal and not persistent. However, there is some agreement that this condition arises from organic factors such as '... genetic variations, biochemical irregularities, perinatal brain insults, illnesses or injuries sustained during the years critical for the development and maturation of the central nervous system or from unknown causes' (Clements, 1966). Recently some attempts have been made to study children so identified through systematic testing. In an investigation by Stevens and his colleagues (1967), children diagnosed as minimally brain-damaged were found to be 'poorer' in every area of performance than were children in the normal group. While stressing the heterogeneity of disordered functioning in this group these investigators concluded 'disorders of attention, attentional impersistence and lack of attentional focus were particularly implicated in the inferior performance of the minimally brain-damaged. These children could attend for just so long and no longer.'

The diagnostic group with which Luria has been concerned included children who, although educationally retarded and behaviourally maladjusted, were intellectually normal. Among the main symptoms shown by this group are distractibility, impulsiveness and a general lack of inhibition. Many of these children were reported as having abnormal births or to have been subjected to early illnesses which may have affected subsequent cerebral development.

Luria (1961) considers the two cardinal symptoms of the *cerebro-aesthenic* syndrome to be a disorder of sustained attention and an impairment in the ability to withhold inappropriate responses. One of the techniques Luria has used to examine cerebro-aesthenic impairment consists of presenting the child with a choice response test in which he is instructed to press a bulb in response to a positive signal and to withhold or inhibit response to a negative signal. The signals used may be visual (different coloured lights) or auditory (bell and buzzer). After a practice period the positive and negative stimuli are presented in random order at different rates of presentation. At rapid rates of presentation the performance of the cerebro-aesthenic child tends to break down and may either fail to respond to any signals or over-respond to both appropriate and inappropriate signals. Although a normal child of a younger age may have difficulty in inhibiting his response in this type of situation, particularly at fast speeds of presentation, the fuller development of the inhibitory processes allow the older child to cope easily with this type of task. In Figure 23 the typical performance of a normal nine-year-old is contrasted with that of a cerebro-aesthenic child of the same age.

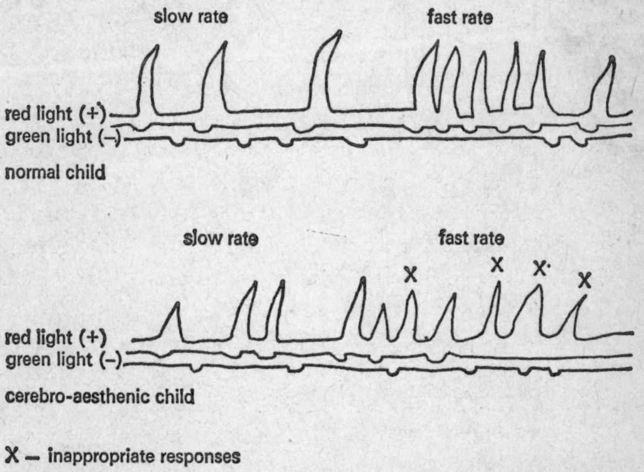

Figure 23 Comparison of normal and cerebro-aesthenic child's motor reactions (Luria, 1961)

The brain-damaged child's failure in this task is not due to an impairment in his ability to discriminate between the two signals, as the child usually shows that he is only too aware of his own inappropriate responses although he is unable to control them. Indeed, the cerebro-aesthenic child can perform the task perfectly well if he is required only to make verbal equivalent responses (e.g. press and don't press) to the positive and negative stimuli. Luria (1963) has demonstrated how the intact verbal responses of the cerebro-aesthenic child may be used to compensate for the lack of inhibition of his motor responses. If the child is encouraged to pronounce the word 'press' and then press the balloon at the presentation of the positive signal and, in response to the inhibitory signal to pronounce the words 'don't press' and refrain from pressing, there is a marked reduction in errors (see Figure 24).

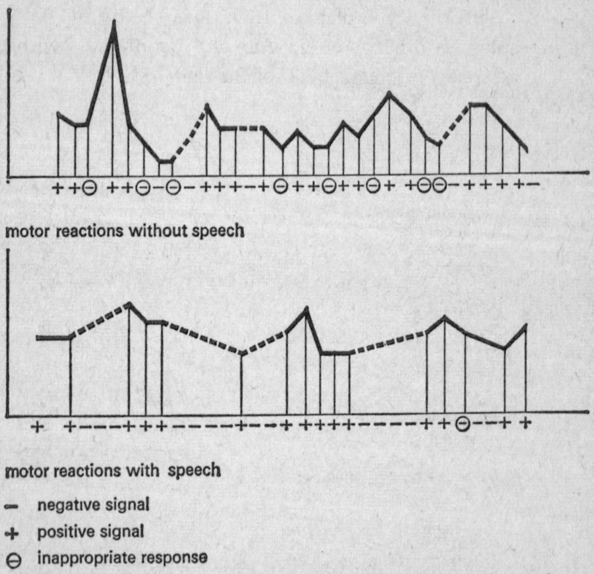

Figure 24 Reaction times of motor responses of cerebro-aesthenic child (Luria, 1963)

Modified forms of Luria's technique have been used to assess personality disturbance in normal school children (Tizard, 1962) and in groups of educationally sub-normal children (Lowe, 1966). In Lowe's study the children taking part were rated by their teachers on Stott's Bristol

Adjustment Guides (1965), a standard rating scale for assessing maladjusted behaviour in children. Children who performed badly on the response inhibition test, giving patterns of response similar to Luria's cerebro-aesthenic children were found to have significantly higher maladjustment scores in the Bristol scale. They were rated by their teachers as being particularly over-impulsive, distractible, aggressive and uncontrolled in their social conduct. In his own work using the Bristol scale, Stott (1960, 1962) extracted a combination of behavioural ratings to form what he termed the *inconsequential syndrome* which he considered to be associated with minimal brain damage. In Lowe's study, children who performed badly on the response inhibition task were found to have high scores on Stott's inconsequential syndrome.

Vigilance

Sustained attention or vigilance has been the subject of many studies in the normal field and, as there seems to be general agreement that the factors operating in vigilance are mainly central in origin, it is surprising how few investigations have been made of signal detection performance in brain-damaged subjects. One such investigation has been reported by McDonald and Burns (1964), who compared the performance of a group of brain-damaged patients with that of hospitalized non-brain-damaged patients on a visual vigilance task requiring the detection and response of variations in dial reflections. It was found that the overall signal detection performance of the brain-damaged group was significantly inferior to that of the controls. The poorer performance of the brain-damaged subjects was particularly evident when signals were presented at a slow rate (twelve critical signals per hour) as opposed to a fast rate (sixty critical signals per hour).

If we interpret the term vigilance rather more loosely than is normal to refer to all tasks where the subject is required to respond to a series of pre-set signals, we may refer to a number of other studies which have examined different aspects of signal detection performance of brain-damaged subjects. The Continuous Performance Test (see page 76) was devised by Rosvold and his colleagues (1956) specifically to provide a measure of changes in sustained attention resulting from brain damage. Rosvold *et al.* (1956) found that groups of brain-damaged adults and children tended to perform at a significantly lower level on this test as compared with non-brain-damaged controls. The poor performance of the brain-damaged subjects was particularly evident in the second A X condition where both attention and short-term retention are involved. A number of other workers using Rosvold's technique have reported considerable success in its discrimination of brain-damaged patients. Schein (1962) used the C.P.T. to successfully discriminate between brain-damaged and other neuropsychiatric patients although he found that some schizophrenic patients tended to give a pattern of responses similar to that associated with brain-damaged patients.

Giving an even more liberal meaning to the term 'vigilance', we might briefly consider the application of reaction-time studies to the assessment of brain damage. A number of reaction-time investigations have demonstrated that the reaction-time latencies of brain-damaged subjects are significantly longer than that of non-brain-damaged controls (Blackburn and Benton, 1955; Benton and Joynt, 1959; Costa, 1962). In the Blackburn and Benton study brain-damaged patients were found to respond at a much slower rate than other non-brain-damaged neurological patients in both simple and choice reaction-time situations. It is of some interest that in this study, choice reaction was found not to be any more discriminative than simple reaction time. Indeed, where differences in discriminative efficiency were found they tended to favour the simple function. More recently De Renzi and Faglioni (1965) assessed the visual reaction times of brain-damaged and non-brain-damaged groups. Their findings substantiated the previous suggestion that simple reaction time provides a reasonably sensitive measurement of generalized brain damage and also suggested that the length of reaction time offers a crude but useful measure of the actual severity of brain damage. De Renzi and Faglioni employed in their study a second 'vigilance' task, a continuous choice reaction test involving not only signal detection but signal discrimination. In this test subjects were required to detect signals appearing on an illuminated visual grid and to respond only to particular combinations of signals (e.g. black circle and a white square) disregarding all other possible combinations of signals. During the test, subjects had before them a visual representation of the correct combination of signals to avoid any retentive difficulties. Although the mean scores of the brain-damaged group were significantly lower than that of the normal control group, further examination demonstrated that this was due mainly to the very poor signal detection performance of brain-damaged patients with aphasic symptoms. Aphasic patients performed fairly well on the test when the signals were presented at a relatively low rate but made many errors when the rate of presentation was increased. While this test is essentially nonverbal in nature, its performance would appear to be aided by internal verbalization which helps the subject both in retaining the detection signal and in stabilizing the perceptive discrimination between closely similar alternative patterns which may appear on the screen.

Attention and apparent movement

Although the investigation of perceptual anomalies is beyond the range of our examination of attentional dysfunctioning, one form of visual illusions has been persistently linked both with attention and brain damage. Reference has already been made (see page 78) to the perception of apparent movement induced by the S.A.E. A number of independent workers have reported a significant reduction or complete absence of the after-effect in patients with known organic cerebral damage. Indeed, the S.A.E. has been reported to give a 98 per cent discrimination between brain-damaged and cerebrally intact groups (Price and Deabler, 1955). Some studies (e.g. Goldberg and Smith, 1958) have confirmed the finding of reduced S.A.E. in brain-damaged subjects although reporting more conservative discriminating indices. However, other investigations report findings in the reverse direction, brain-damaged patients showing a stronger after-effect of longer duration. Spivack and Levine (1957; 1959) found that a longer S.A.E. discriminated brain-damaged from normal subjects and that this effect was independent of age, intelligence, memory deficit or of measures of other forms of visual illusions. Some studies have reported a tendency for brain-damaged subjects to experience a reduced after-effect but have not found this tendency marked enough to differentiate reliably mixed organic and normal groups (Holland and Beech, 1958). Others (Page, Rakita, Kaplan and Smith, 1957) failed to find any differences between brain-damaged and control groups in the duration of after-effect.

In his detailed review of investigations of this illusion, Holland (1965) has drawn attention to the relatively unstandardized scoring procedures used and the probability that vagaries in scoring might account for some of the contradictory findings reported. Most investigations have depended upon the verbal report of the subject as to the presence and duration of the after-effect. However, Scott, Bragg and Smarr (1963) have devised a modified form of the technique which lends itself to more objective scoring. Using this more rigid scoring system Scott found that the S.A.E. still differentiated brain-damaged from normal subjects at about a 94 per cent level of discrimination. Holland (1965) is of the opinion that past findings of the discriminatory functions of this technique with brain-damaged patients must be cautiously interpreted until it has been more thoroughly standardized.

Even if differences in the S.A.E. of brain-damaged

patients are confirmed and established, the question remains as to how such differences may be interpreted. Most studies which report positive discriminatory findings assume that the perceptual anomaly is the direct expression of cerebral impairment. However, recent studies by Efstathiou and Morant (1966) suggest that this assumption may be unwarranted. The after-effect of perceived movement depends upon adequate fixation of the spiral during its rotation. Although the influence of fixation and eye movement upon S.A.E. performance has been considered by some workers (e.g. Holland, 1965), such variables have not been systematically examined before. Efstathiou and Morant (1966) employed a technique where subjects were encouraged to fix the centre of the moving spiral and found that these instructions greatly increased the incidence of the after-effect in brain-damaged subjects. In a second experiment where subjects were sometimes instructed to fix the periphery of the spiral, a group of normal subjects all returned scores which would usually be taken to be indicative of brain damage. In their second paper Morant and Efstathiou (1966) confirmed their previous findings by comparing the performance of brain-damaged subjects on the S.A.E. and the waterfall after-effect. The latter illusion of reverse movement is obtained as an after-effect of viewing a moving set of parallel lines. As the waterfall illusion is unidirectional the after-effect is independent upon the part of the waterfall figure fixated. It was thus hypothesized that brain-damaged patients should perform significantly better on this latter illusion than one the S.A.E., where central fixation is an important determinant. This suggestion was confirmed in their subsequent experiment. It should be pointed out that Efstathiou and Morant's findings are based upon the presence or absence of the after-effect and not upon differences in its duration. However, it appears likely that the reports of poor performance of brain-damaged patients on the S.A.E. may be partially due to the poorer attentiveness of such patients.

Attentional Dysfunction in Specific Categories of Brain Damage

Most of the preceding studies have examined brain-damaged groups as a homogeneous diagnostic category in spite of the logical absurdity of such a view. Perhaps the main reason for this self-imposed limitation lies in the difficulty of accurately locating a brain lesion even when detailed pathological information is available from post-mortem examination. In diagnosing a localized lesion the clinician will of course call upon his own experience and clinical skill, and upon the information provided by ancillary techniques such as E.E.G. reports, skull radiology, and other detailed neurological assessments. Such information may be of great value in diagnosing the location of the primary foci but it can also be misleading. Damage to one part of the brain may produce E.E.G. changes in other regions. A primary lesion in one cerebral area may cause secondary damage in other adjacent areas, the observation of which may be masked by the main lesion. Finally, although there does appear to be a reasonable association between the extensiveness of damage and behavioural changes (Corsellis, 1962), the level of the association is not always high. Some patients show only slight behavioural deterioration although subsequent post-mortem examination may reveal severe and extensive brain damage. Nevertheless, while identification of psychological functions with particular structures in the brain and central nervous system may be unwarranted by our present limited knowledge, some studies would appear to offer useful suggestions of possible correlations between function and structure.

Before examining studies of localized focal lesions we might first discuss pathologies of attention in the more diffuse form of brain disease occurring in the senile psychoses.

Senile psychoses

Although senile dementia has a relatively high incidence,

and accounts for an increasing proportion of the mental hospital population, the advanced age and poor prognosis of its members make it a self-limiting problem. This may be one explanation why senile psychosis has been comparatively neglected by psychological research workers. The need for research is particularly pronounced in the area of attentional dysfunction where practically no systematic studies have been reported. However, as many of the symptoms of senile dementia present as exaggerated forms of the changes in mental functioning occurring in normal senescence, studies of attentional changes in ageing have obvious relevance to future research in this fied. The ageing process has been the subject of exhaustive experimental research but we shall restrict ourselves to a brief summary of a few studies which have special significance to senile dementia.

It is a common observation that elderly people have difficulty in sustaining their attention for any period of time and one might therefore expect that vigilance tasks would show a marked deficit in performance with age. However, most of the studies report that age has surprisingly little effect on either visual (York, 1962) or auditory (Griew and Davies, 1962) vigilance performance. The few studies which have found a decline in vigilance in older subjects have involved factors other than sustained attention. In the Griew and Davies (1962) study, subjects were presented with a series of tape recorded digits and required to respond by key-pressing each time they detected three consecutive odd numbers. Under this condition no age differences were found whether the signals were presented at a slow (twenty-four per hour) or fast (sixty-six per hour) rate of presentation. However, when the instructions were altered to require the subject to indicate his detection of the relevant signal by writing down the three consecutive digits, older subjects performed badly. It appeared that the very act of writing down the digits interrupted their attention and increased the load on short-term memory. During the act of responding the subsequent auditory signals would presumably act as distractors. It is of course a well-established finding that short-term memory tends to decline with age. Indeed Welford (1958) has suggested that the decrease in storage capacity represents one of the most important and far-reaching senescent changes. A number of investigations of this decline have demonstrated that, when a task involving short-term memory is combined with a secondary distracting task, older subjects tend to perform badly in at least one of the tasks (Broadbent and Heron, 1962). Younger adults are unable to deal with two tasks simultaneously unless the informational content of one of the tasks is near zero. However, they may be able to cope with two tasks successively by rapidly alternating their attention between the two tasks. One set of data may be held for a brief period in the short-term memory store while the other set of data is being processed. Inefficient performance of elderly patients on tasks demanding the switching of attention may then be due to an impairment in short-term retention or to a slowing down in the *rate* at which information is processed. (These two phenomena are obviously not independent.)

A reduction in the response speed is perhaps the best documented of the changes in mental processes occurring in later life. Although such slowing down in mental output may be partially explained in terms of peripheral deterioration of the sense organs and effectors, it is now clear that the basic cause of the slowing has a more central origin within the brain. Reaction-time studies (e.g. Birren and Bottwinck, 1955) have made it clear that the marked slowing down in reaction time with age is only minimally due to a slowing in the conductive rate of peripheral nerves. Neurophysiological work has now established that advancing years bring an increasing reduction in the number of cells functioning in the brain. This atrophying process might be expected to cause a decrease in the rate of the central conduction of information in the brain and central nervous system. It has also been suggested that there is an increase in random electrical activity in the brain (neural noise) during senescence, which tends to mask the registration of incoming signals. Finally, there is some evidence from E.E.G. studies that in old age the cerebral activity induced by incoming signals has a longer lasting 'echo' effect than in earlier years and that this increases the possibility of the registration of one signal input exerting a pro-active inhibitory effect upon the registration of subsequent signals. This effect has been demonstrated in brain-damaged patients in Birch's work which we considered earlier in this chapter.

Reaction-time tasks provide the simplest method of measuring the processing rate and there has been no shortage of studies employing this procedure with older subjects. Such studies are unanimous in their agreement that both auditory and visual reaction time increases with age. Although this increase in latency applies to both simple and complex reaction-time tasks, the age decrement in performance is most evident in the latter situation involving both switching of attention and decision making. Talland (1963) used available information of changes in brain weight with age to give an approximate index of active brain cells occurring at different age periods. Although brain weight is an exceedingly crude representation of brain cell atrophy it does give some idea of the amount of cerebral decay. When the reciprocal values of mean brain weight in successive decades were plotted on a graph together with appropriate measures of changes in simple and disjunctive visual reaction time, the curves suggested that increase in disjunctive reaction time with age closely parallels the indirect measure of decay rate of brain cells with age (see Figure 25).

The E.E.G. has frequently been employed as a means of timing the registration of signals in the brain and, less directly, as a measure of attention variability in old age. Records of the brain activity of elderly subjects show a decline in fast and an increase in slow frequency rhythms. These E.E.G. changes are particularly pronounced in

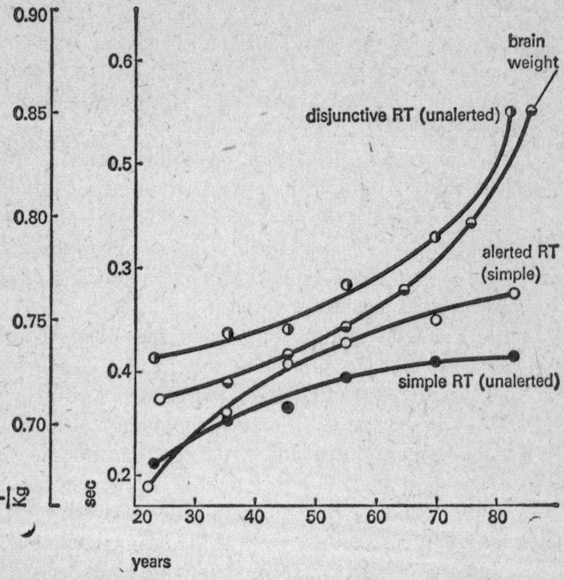

Figure 25 Age changes in reaction time and brain weight (Talland, 1963)

elderly patients with diffuse brain damage and the association between slow frequency of neural activity and intellectual deterioration allows the E.E.G. to be of some limited use in charting the course of such conditions as senile dementia. Figure 26 illustrates a typical comparison of two groups of normal and demented elderly subjects where it can be seen that the patient group show a displacement towards slow and neural activity.

There is some evidence to suggest that the slowing down of reaction time in old age is associated with the presence of slow brain potential in the E.E.G. In one investigation (Surwillo, 1961) E.E.G. records were made while subjects were performing a reaction-time experiment. Significantly high positive correlations (+0·72) were found between mean length of reaction time and mean duration of the

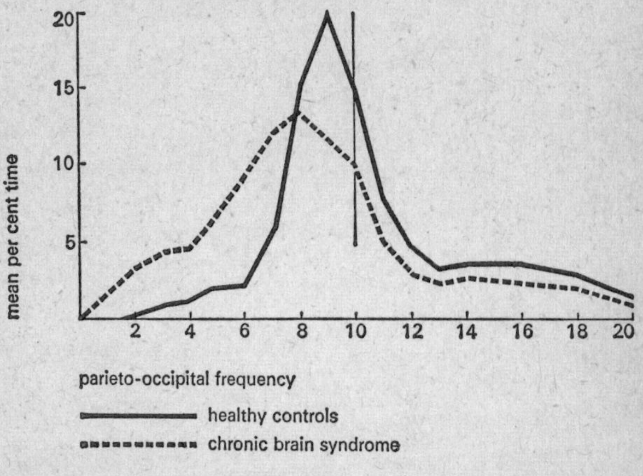

Figure 26 Comparison of E.E.G. records of normal and demented elderly groups (Obrist, 1963)

E.E.G. waves. Surwillo also demonstrated that the positive correlation between reaction time and age disappears when E.E.G. frequencies are controlled. Blocking or desynchronization of the E.E.G. alpha rhythm has been frequently represented as a measure of attention or arousal, on the grounds that alpha desynchronization is the result of impulses from the reticular system raising the level of cortical excitation. Several studies have revealed that elderly subjects show less desynchronization to visual light stimuli than younger age groups and that this is even more pronounced in elderly patients with organic brain disease (e.g. Wells, 1962). The falling off in E.E.G. reactivity in old age was again confirmed in a study by Wilson and Obrist (1963) who also compared the habituation rate of elderly and young subjects to a repeated visual stimulus. Their results suggest that older people show a similar rate of habituation as younger people, but less reactivity to signals (see Figure 27). Commenting on their own results Wilson and Obrist (1963) observe – 'It is as if the elderly person came into the experiment already

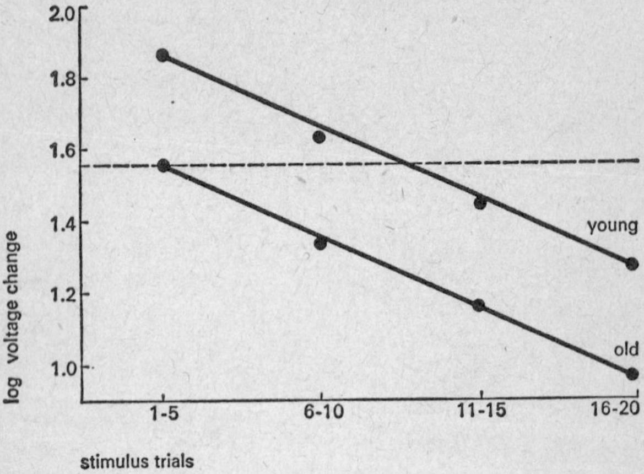

Figure 27 Habituation of arousal response in younger and older subjects (Wilson and Obrist, 1963)

partially adapted at a level corresponding to the tenth trial of the younger group ...'

There has been a great deal of speculation regarding the possible reason behind the characteristic slowing down of information processing in old age. If, as the above work suggests, older people are less cortically aroused, this might be one factor in the slowing process. The evidence that the rate of neural transmission from the senses to the brain is reduced with age and that signal registration exerts a greater and longer lasting inhibiting effect on the registration of immediately subsequent input would seem to point to another related cause. A third possibility has been raised by work which suggests that older people are less able to monitor input for informational redundancy. If the pattern of incoming signals contains elements which are predictable, the determinateness of these elements may be utilized to reduce the amount of decision making involved in the task. Some studies have indicated that elderly people are less able to utilize such redundancies so that they are in the position of having to process more information than younger subjects. This relative inability to screen out redundant or irrelevant information is well illustrated by an experiment reported by Rabbitt (1963). The material used in this experiment consisted of sets of cards bearing one to nine letters, one of which was always the letter A or Z. Subjects were required to sort the cards into two piles, depending on whether the card contained an A or Z. The amount of irrelevant information varied in different sortings, depending upon the number of letters other than As or Zs appearing in the cards in the pack (see Figure 28).

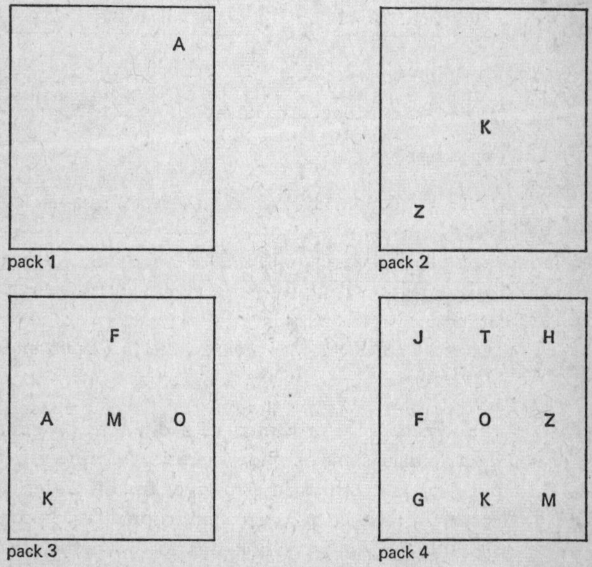

Figure 28 Example of cards used in sorting task (Rabbitt, 1963)

It was found that older subjects showed a significant increase in the time taken to sort the packs with every increase in the number of irrelevant signals contained in the cards. Rabbitt interpreted his findings as suggesting that older people require to sample a wider range of cues before disregarding these as redundant. The slowing down in their performance is thus due to their need to use more information than younger subjects before discriminating between the relevant and redundant signals. Further evidence of poor 'redundancy stripping' in older people is provided in a more recent experiment by Rabbitt and Birren (1967) using a visuo-motor device called a 'psychomet'. The apparatus consists of a panel containing a row of ten circular lamps, each operative being set above a contact grid which switched off its lamps when touched lightly (see Figure 29).

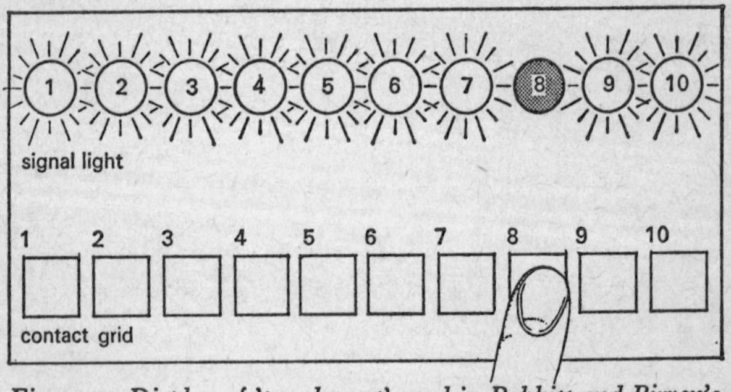

Figure 29 Display of 'psychomet' used in Rabbitt and Birren's (1967) study

Subjects were presented with different programmes of light signals, some of which were repetitive (e.g. 4-5-6-4-5-6-4-5-6) and others interruptive. In this latter category, recurrent sequences were interrupted unexpectedly by signals. The subject's task was to touch the appropriate contact grid as soon as any lamp was lighted. It was found that subjects over the age of sixty years, although slower on the continuous sequence programmes, made fewer errors when the sequence was changed by the appearance of an interruptive signal. Younger subjects soon learned the nature of repetitive sequences and therefore did not find it necessary to identify each signal in a sequence (e.g.

in a 4-5-6 sequence the identification of lamp 4 being lit was sufficient information to allow grids 4, 5 and 6 to be tapped without any further decision making). The younger person's ability to screen out the redundancy in the task greatly increased their speed of response as compared with that of the older person who found it necessary to identify and respond to each signal separately. However, when a sequence was interrupted unexpectedly the strategy of the younger person acted to his disadvantage while the slower signal processing of the older person rendered him less likely to be 'caught napping'.

These results raise one final question in regard to the performance of the older person on any type of task. It is often said that, although the older worker may be slower, he is more accurate and reliable. Most experimental studies of changes in different skills with age confirm that older people tend to compensate for their slower speed of reaction by increased attention to accuracy. A premium on accuracy rather than speed may also be influenced by personal and social factors combining to make the older person less confident in his own ability and more aware of the possibility of error. This suggestion of changing levels of confidence in old age introduces a variable which is extremely difficult to bring under experimental control and which may exert a powerful but little known influence on all studies of performance in senescence. Presented with a series of positive and negative signals, the younger person may adopt the strategy of responding to all signals which are at all likely to be positive. This may increase the number of false positive responses but will ensure a fast performance. The older person may be more inclined to adopt a more cautious strategy, only identifying signals of which he is certain, so greatly slowing down his performance. Although confidence levels and speed of identification and processing are obviously connected, there are sufficient differences between them to prevent a too ready assignment of old age decrements to central impairments in the brain and nervous system. The point at issue has been well summarized in Rabbitt's (1963) warning to those who are tempted to view the elderly person as an irreparable over-used computer:

> One may compare the ageing organism to a disabled analog computer, whose capacity for carrying out programmes is increasingly limited as components fail. The range of the computer's performance will be determined by both the total and the specific loss of components, but these losses can be circumvented to some degree by alternative programming, allowing the best use of existing potential ... While the logical structure of a programme is related to events in the computer's circuitry, and the circuitry determines the choice of operation available to the programme this correspondence is not complete ... In the common behaviour of everyday life, adequate criteria for the quantification of performance – data have not been established ... In tasks of this type the human being must be regarded as choosing between a repertory of possible strategies. It is possible that with increasing age this repertory diminishes; but the choice between strategies will still be determined to a great degree by the subject's personal experience ... To behave as though the translation from neurology to performance were unmodified by the life experience of an organism would repeat the error of confusing a computer's programme with its hardware (Rabbitt, 1963).

We have spent some time considering changes in attention in normal senescence, because it seems likely that such studies can provide a secure and useful foundation for investigating the pathologies of attention occurring in senile dementia. Very few systematic studies of attentional dysfunction in senile patients have been reported. Williams (1956) carried out a study of the visual perceptual performance of a group of senile dementia patients with a matched group of non-demented elderly patients. In several experiments she demonstrated that the slow and inaccurate perceptual performance of the demented patients was due mainly to their inability to select the appropriate and inhibit the irrelevant cues in the perceptual field. In her final conclusion she argues that '... what the demented patient lacks is not so much the ability to behave in a fitting manner as the ability to select from his environment the cues to tell what is fitting. It is not so much that he is unable to receive information through his senses, but that he is unable to select or abstract from all the information available that which is relevant' (Williams, 1956). This statement has striking similarities with that made by Rabbitt and Birren in their study of the effects of normal senescence: '... the old may take longer than the young to discriminate between complex stimuli because they pay attention to aspects of the stimuli (cues) which are irrelevant or redundant ... Young people seem to consider fewer cues and select better than the old between those which are relevant and those which are redundant or misleading' (Rabbitt and Birren, 1967). A similar tendency of distractibility by irrelevant cues was noted in the elderly arteriosclerotic patients compared with schizophrenic patients in the study reported by Lawson, McGhie and Chapman (1967) (see page 96). The inability of the arteriosclerotic patients to deal with redundancy was also evident in their failure to use the contextual constraints of language in reproducing passages of varying degrees of redundancy (Lawson, 1965). McGhie and his colleagues are at present engaged in a detailed longitudinal study of elderly demented patients, involving repeated assessments of changes in attention, learning, memory psychomotor and intellectual performance of patients and normal elderly control subjects. Although this study is still in progress, and the data from its first phase not yet fully analysed, it is already evident that the elderly demented patients are distinguished by their slowness to process information and their inability to reduce the information load by discarding redundancy. Using the Continuous Performance Test, for example, it is evident that the non-demented elderly subject greatly simplifies his task by ignoring letters which are perceptually different from the target signal X (e.g. such letters as C, O, P may be dismissed as redundant on the basis of their curvilinearity).

In contrast to this, the demented patient has to identify each signal separately (often naming the letter aloud) before deciding if it is an X which requires a response. Some of the more recently developed work on visual search would seem to offer excellent techniques for examining this relationship between redundancy discrimination and speed of performance in more detail.

Research into dementia in old age is made more complex by the difficulty in selecting matched normal controls. Many of the elderly subjects in the normal population who agree to act as controls are found to be as demented (both clinically and on the basis of their test performance) as the senile hospital patients constituting the experimental groups. We have already discussed the point that hospital admission and subsequent labelling of senile dementia is often a result of social pressures rather than an indication of the functioning level of the individual. It is nevertheless difficult to understand how it is possible for some elderly people to live apparently relatively independent and well-adjusted lives in their community while their performance on a variety of psychological tests suggests that their capacity to make rational judgement is so severely impaired. Much remains to be known regarding the non-cognitive factors which may apparently compensate for very severe levels of dementia.

Temporal lobe lesions

Most psychological studies of the effects of damage to the temporal lobes of the brain have substantiated the earlier suggestion by Penfield (1954b) and others that the most important function of this region of the brain is the storage of memories. The majority of these studies agree that, while unilateral temporal lobe damage has little effect on memory, extensive damage to both temporal lobes can have a profound effect on storage capacity. These findings have been further extended by investigations which point to the hippocampal area of the temporal lobes as dealing with the short-term phases of memory. Milner and Penfield (1955) have suggested that, as bilateral hippocampal damage tends to affect the short-term storing of data before it is 'consolidated' in the more permanent long-term store. A more recent investigation of the storage functions of the hippocampal area stresses its role in allowing attention to be switched between different stimuli. In this study Stepien and Sierpinski (1960) utilized a simple but effective technique to measure changes in short-term retention. Subjects were presented with pairs of visual stimuli of different degrees of brightness or with pure auditory tones of different pitches. The subject's task was simply to press a key when the two signals were perceived as being identical (in brightness or tone). In order to avoid problems of individual differences in discriminability, differences between the signals when they did occur were large. By extending the interval between the two signals up to a limit of two minutes, the technique allows a satisfactory measure of the efficiency of short-term retention. In a second condition, this technique was repeated with the interval between the two signals filled with a distracting stimulus. The results of applying this procedure to temporal-lobe-damaged patients were in accordance with the findings of other investigations, namely that unilateral damage leaves performance unimpaired while bilateral damage produces a marked impairment in short-term retention. This effect was clearly demonstrated in some patients who were tested before and after removal of epileptogenic foci in both temporal lobes. The poor preoperative performance of such patients was superseded by a normal level of performance after surgical removal of the source of the abnormality. Stepien and Sierpinski found that the impact of the distracting stimulus was particularly marked with bilateral damage to the hippocampal area and interpreted this as suggesting that 'this area plays an important role in preserving the recent memory traces when the person turns his attention to something else.'

Other studies imply that there are hemispherical differences in the functions of the two temporal lobes, the dominant lobe being concerned with the storage of verbal auditory material, and the non-dominant lobe dealing with the storage of visual non-verbal material (Milner, 1958; Kimura, 1966).

The import of these and other studies indicates that the two temporal lobes have somewhat different functions in respect of their modality specialization. Such differences in function may explain why a high degree of learning capacity may remain even after the loss of one temporal lobe. Presumably subsequent learning is mediated mainly in the alternative sensory channels. If both lobes are extensively damaged or removed, retention of information in both modalities is affected and learning severely impaired. Attentional disorders such as heightened distractibility are evident in temporal-lobe-damaged patients only in situations involving the short-term retention of information.

Frontal lobe lesions

The frontal lobes of the brain have been traditionally regarded as the seat of man's higher mental functions. The use of frontal lobe surgery in treating some severe forms of mental illness presented an indirect opportunity for further study of this large area of the brain and for some time it appeared that this area was important for adequate intellectual functioning. However, subsequent, more carefully controlled studies of changes in intellectual performance following psychosurgery have failed to confirm this suggestion and there is at present no convincing evidence to connect the frontal lobes with intelligence. As frontal-lobe-damaged patients are commonly observed to be excessively uninhibited in their behaviour, the possibility arises that the frontal area is concerned with controlling behaviour. This suggestion implicates attentional factors in that one aspect of inhibition is the screening out of irrelevant stimuli. A number of studies (e.g. Maher,

Elder and Noblin, 1962) have demonstrated that the destruction of frontal lobe tissue in animals causes the animal to be hyperdistractible to any fluctuation in environmental stimulation. Loss of inhibition following frontal lobe damage has also been reported by Rosvold and Mishkin (1961) using a conditioning technique with dogs. The technique involves a response being established to one conditioned stimulus and the inhibition of the same response being established to an alternative conditioned stimulus. After frontal lobe surgery the excitatory (positive) response is magnified while the inhibitory response is reduced or disappears completely. (The dog gives the excitatory response to both the positive and negative stimuli.) If similar surgery is directed to other parts of the brain (e.g. parietal lobes) this disinhibitory effect is not observed. Campbell and Harlow (1945) have summarized their conclusions of the effect of frontal lobe damage in monkeys as follows – 'following the destruction of the frontal and pre-frontal association areas (they) suffer a deficit in attending and fixating limited aspects of a test situation ...'

A similar failure in inhibition in human patients with frontal lobe lesions has been reported by Luria and his colleagues. Using a variation of the two-choice discrimination task employed in his work with cerebro-aesthenic children, Luria (1960) has demonstrated the frontal lobe patient's deficit in response inhibition. If asked to press a bulb strongly in response to a red light and to press it gently or refrain from pressing in response to a green light the patient presses with equal strength to both signals. This failure is not due to his being unable to understand the requirements of the task, as he is able to verbalize the correct response (i.e. he correctly identifies the signal by saying 'red – press' or (green – don't press') although he is unable to inhibit his subsequent motor response. Luria's colleague Khomskaya (1965) found that, whereas normal subjects show a quick reinstatement of habituated orienting response in response to verbal instructions, similar instructions fail to reinstate the orienting response in patients with frontal lobe lesions. This inability to verbally direct orienting response is not observed in patients with lesions in other areas of the brain.

Several other studies have examined the effect of frontal lobe injury on the distribution of attention between two sets of stimuli. Rylander (1939) used two simple tests of attention (cancelling letters and adding columns of numbers) with a frontal-lobe-damaged group under conditions of distraction and no distraction. The distracting stimulus was a metronome and the subjects were required to interrupt their performance on the main cancelling or adding task to indicate their awareness of brief pauses in the metronome clicks. Rylander found that the distracting stimulus greatly reduced the speed of performance of the frontal lobe patients on the main task. Later Walch (1958) found the same results using a very similar technique. In another study of patients before and after prefrontal leucotomy, Costello (1956) investigated the frontal lobe patient's ability to attend and respond to two sets of data simultaneously. His procedure employed a modified version of a test used earlier by Rylander. In this test the subject is presented with a card bearing a number of meaningless figures, one of which occurs twice in different positions. The subject is then required to find this identical figure on a multiple choice card (identification) and to indicate on another card the positions occupied by the repeated figure in the original card (localization) (see Figure 30).

Costello found that, while the patient who had undergone frontal lobe surgery was able to cope with the task when asked to *either* identify *or* localize the repeated figures, he was unable to cope when asked to do both simultaneously. Costello interpreted his results to indicate that the frontal lobe patient shows a deficiency in maintaining two modes of response simultaneously.

The frontal lobes of the brain occupy a relatively large area of the cortex and there is no reason why they should

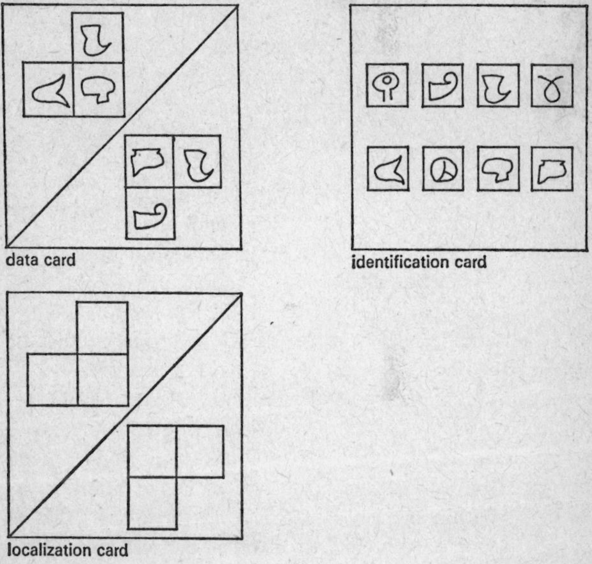

Figure 30 Examples of three categories of cards used in Costello's (1956) study

be regarded as homogeneous structures. There is already some evidence that the failure of inhibiting responses already described is associated with lesions of the basal parts of the lobes. Luria has suggested that deeper lesions of the mesial parts of the frontal lobe, with its connexions with subcortical and limbic structures, may result in disturbances of vigilance and to what he refers to as 'impaired selectivity'. A recent paper (Luria, Homskaya, Blinkov and Critchley, 1967) includes an extensive examination of the changes produced by a deep frontal lesion. The patient concerned showed a severe defect of sustained attention and was involuntarily engaged by an extraneous stimulus. Faced with any situation involving a choice between uncertain alternatives he was completely unable to bring any selective attention to bear on the problem. The possible involvement of the brain-stem reticular system in such deep frontal damage makes it difficult to judge the extent to which subcortical rather than frontal-lobe damage contributes to such a marked impairment in sustained attention.

Sub-cortical lesions

Although the anatomical and physiological components of the brain-stem recticular-activating system are still somewhat diffuse, there seems little doubt that this is a vital part of the nervous system for the maintenance of attention. A number of psychological studies of patients with sub-cortical lesions have substantiated the view that the maintenance of attention is partly dependent upon the integrity of central sub-cortical structures. In a study of visual monitoring (McDonald and Burns, 1964), it was found that the error rate of signal selection in patients with sub-cortical injuries was three times that of patients with lesions located in other cortical areas. In two independent investigations by Mirsky *et al.* (1960) and Landsell and Mirsky (1964) both employing the Continuous Performance Test, patients with centrencephalic epilepsy were reported to make many more errors than patients whose epilepsy had a cortical focus. Kimura (1964) has also compared centrencephalic and cortically damaged epileptics on a letter-ordering task requiring subjects to report in alphabetical order a series of randomly presented letters. Again, a lower performance was evident in those patients with sub-cortical damage.

These and other related findings have been interpreted as supporting the general hypothesis that the maintenance of attention is dependent upon the integrity of central sub-cortical structures.

Summary and Conclusions

The examination of the effects of brain damage on attention is beset with ambiguities and difficulties. Some of these difficulties arise from the vagaries inherent in the clinical diagnosis and assessment of brain damage while others reflect the permeable boundaries between attention and other mental processes. The possibility of aphasic symptoms in such cases introduces another variable which may exert a hidden influence on performance on both verbal and non-verbal tests of attention. While there would appear to be a fair measure of agreement that brain-damaged subjects are more distractible than individuals with intact cerebral structures, the overinclusive nature of distractibility greatly limits the usefulness of this conclusion. It would seem that distraction effects are most evident in tasks which demand a meaningful response to the secondary distracting stimulus so that the main deficit may be a relative inability to alternate attention between two sets of data in proximity. There is some fairly convincing evidence that this form of attentional dysfunction is partially due to a slowing down in the rate at which information is processed when certain cerebral areas are impaired. The lowered efficiency in monitoring information for redundant elements may exert a contributory influence on the reduced rate of processing in causing the brain-damaged patient to deal with a greater amount of information per unit of time than is normaly processed. Another aspect of the failure to switch attention at an adequate rate is seen in the impulsive errors made by brain-damaged patients on tests demanding a discriminatory control of response. Current reports suggest that such failure in response inhibition may be more specificially linked with frontal-lobe damage. On theoretical grounds it might be expected that subcortical damage would cause the most pronounced changes in attention, and further investigation of the results of such lesions may increase our understanding of the relationship between the functional and structural components of attention. However, more precise measurements in this area are likely to continue to be hindered by the complexities of localizing sub-cortical lesions and by our limited understanding of the neurophysiological interaction of sub-cortical and cortical structures.

6 Mental Deficiency (Subnormality)

The Clinical Picture

This diagnostic category lies outside the range of psychiatric syndromes hitherto considered since it does not imply the presence of neurotic, psychotic or any other psychopathological symptoms. The subnormal person's deficit is limited to his intellectual development although the severity of this deficit is likely to effect his capacity to adjust to his environment. Although under the Mental Health Act of 1959 intellectual deficit is a necessary criterion for the diagnosis of subnormality, the adequacy of the individual's adjustment to society is regarded as a deciding factor in deciding whether or not institutional care is advised. Under the new Act the former sub-division of mental deficiency into the three grades of feeblemindedness, imbecility and idiocy is replaced by the simpler two-fold division of subnormality and severe subnormality. It has been suggested (*Report of B.P.S. Working Party on Subnormality*, 1963; McKerracher and Scott, 1966) that an I.Q. level of 55 (three standard deviations from the mean) should be taken as a demarcation point between the two levels of subnormality. This division between subnormality and severe subnormality may also be made on purely clinical grounds, the former category being seen to contain the 'sub-cultural' defectives who differ only in degree from the rest of the normal population. These individuals diagnosed as being severely subnormal may be regarded as differing qualitatively from the normal population in that their intellectual deficiency is due to brain damage resulting from brain injury at birth or to genetic anomalies. This approach has frequently led research workers to make the rather dubious assumption that a low I.Q. (usually under 55) may be regarded as sufficient evidence of brain damage.

Experimental Studies

Theories of attentional deficit in subnormality

A number of psychological studies have suggested that the primary impairment in the learning of subnormal individuals occurs at the first input stage of the process. In Britain the work of O'Connor and Hermelin (1963) and others has laid great stress on poor short-term retention as an important feature in the subnormal learning. A similar conclusion is evident in the work of American psychologists such as Ellis (1963) who postulates that the subnormal brain is distinguished by a lowered capacity to initiate and maintain the reverberatory neural circuits necessary for efficient short-term storage. Ellis has put forward a variety of experimental findings in support of his theory that the duration and intensity of the stimulus trace (initially in the form of a reverberatory circuit) is weakened in the subnormal organism thus causing a low level of performance on tasks involving short-term storage. Another attempt to explain subnormality in terms of impairment at the in-put stage has been made by Spitz (1963) who suggested that subnormal individuals show a reduction in *cortical satiation*. Spitz's hypothesis is that the perception of a stimulus causes an electrochemical change in the projection area of the brain which temporarily blocks or *satiates* subsequent stimulation. Spitz has interpreted a variety of experimental findings as evidence of reduced satiation in subnormality due to impaired brain-cell functioning.

Other theories of the subnormal learning process locate the main impairment directly at the initial phase of attention. Zeaman and House have carried out a number of studies of discriminative learning in subnormal subjects which convince them that the basic deficit in the subnormal individual is an attentional one. Summarizing their findings and those of other workers, Zeaman and House (1963) argue that

> the visual discriminative learning of moderately retarded children requires the acquisition of a chain of two responses:
> (1) attending to the relative stimulus dimensions, and
> (2) approaching the correct cues of that dimension.
> The difficulty that retardates have in discriminative learning is related to limitations in the first, or attentional, phase of this dual process rather than the second.

Zeaman and House have used a standard discriminative learning procedure to investigate the manner in which subnormal children can be trained to discriminate at different levels of complexity between two simultaneously presented visual stimuli. Using this technique to investigate a variety of factors affecting discriminative learning, Zeaman and House reach the conclusion that the *rate* of learning is not a crucial factor in distinguishing the performance of subnormal and normal children. The subnormal child learns as quickly as other children *if* he is able (or is specifically taught) to attend to the relevant aspects of the discriminative problem. On this basis it is suggested that the most successful educational approach to the subnormal child is likely to be that which seeks to increase the attentional value of the relevant cues and so allow the process of discriminative learning to proceed in a more normal manner.

Zeaman and House (1963) conclude their summary of their own work by suggesting that, although their studies of the attentional deficit in subnormals have been retricted to visual discriminative learning, they see no reason why a similar impairment in attention should not be found in other types of situations. In the remaining part of this section we will examine the extent to which findings of other studies, utilizing different approaches, support the view that attentional deficit is an important feature of subnormality.

Stimulus intensity and attention

If the type of attentional deficit postulated in the Zeaman and House theory is correct it might be expected that an increase in the intensity of stimulus presentation would lead to an improvement in subnormal learning. The effects of varying stimulus intensity have been studied by a number of workers whose findings tend to support the Zeaman and House viewpoint. O'Connor and Hermelin (1963) introduced this attentional variable in a comparative study of word associate learning in severely subnormal (imbecile) adults and normal subjects of a similar mental age (six-year-old children). No differences were evident either in long-term memory or in learning between the subnormal and normal subjects, most differences between the groups being confined to short-term recall. The subnormal subjects, however, required significantly more presentations before learning began and learning was also faster and more efficient if the relevant stimuli were presented at a higher degree of auditory intensity. Surveying the results of several of their experimental studies of subnormal learning O'Connor and Hermelin (1963) conclude

Thus the evidence points to deficits in acquisition rather than poor perception, retention or transfer ability. Acquisition seems to be impaired at least partly because of an inability to focus attention on the relevant stimulus features . . . In other words, the imbecile cannot begin to learn until he has found out what precisely it is that he should learn. . . .

Other studies have experimented on the effects of increasing the intensity of the preparatory signals on the reaction time of subnormal subjects. Such investigations are partly based on the Zeaman and House attentional deficit model but also reflect the allied hypothesis that subnormals are habitually at a lower level of arousal than normals and that therefore conditions designed to increase alertness should facilitate response time. Baumeister, Hawkins and Koenigsknecht (1965) studied the alerting effect of warning signals or visual reaction time of subnormals. The subjects in this investigation were a group of cultural-familial defective adults and normal subjects matched for chronological age. The reaction signal was a red light to which the subject responded verbally (through a throat microphone) with the word 'red'. The warning signal consisted either of a white light or buzzer, or of both the visual and auditory signals in conjunction, and three lengths of preparatory intervals were involved. Although the reaction time latencies of the subnormal group were significantly slower than that of the normals, the hypothesized more alerting signal (light and buzzer) did not facilitate the performance of the subnormal subjects. As the preparatory intervals used in this experiment were rather long (up to eight seconds) the study was repeated using shorter intervals to ensure that any alerting quality of the warning signal was not being dissipated before the appearance of the reaction signal. As once again the alerting signal had no apparent effect on the reaction times of the subnormal subjects it was concluded that readiness to respond probably consists of a motor set which is little influenced by the level of activation.

An alternative explanation for the negative findings of Baumeister *et al.* (1965) might be that the alerting value of the light and buzzer in conjunction was no higher than that of either signal alone. To investigate this possibility the experiment was repeated gauging the effects of varying the intensity of a visual warning signal on the visual reaction time of subnormals (Hawkins, Baumeister and Holland, 1965). Contrary to the expectations of the Zeaman and House arousal model of subnormality, it was found that increasing the intensity of the visual warning signal elicited a *slower* reaction time. Hawkins and his colleagues suggest that the *absolute* intensity of the warning signal is less important than the *relative* differences in intensities between the warning and reaction signals. After an intense warning signal the perceived intensity of the reaction signal may be reduced and therefore less well discriminated than in conditions where the reaction signal follows a relatively weak warning signal. This view might appear to contradict Spitz's theory of *reduced* cortical satiation which infers that a relatively intense visual warning signal would have less rather than more effect on subnormal reaction time. However, the contradiction is more apparent than real as Spitz (1963) has made it plain that his concept of satiation is a fatigue process (allied to Hull's reactive inhibition), resulting from *repeated* or *lengthy* stimulation of one cortical area. In any event, the absence of normal control data in the above study does not allow us to assess the effect of intensifying the warning signal on normal subjects. These experimental data may, however, be interpreted as supporting Birch's contention (see chapter 5) that any form of brain damage reduces both the rate of information processing and the time taken for recovery from previous stimulation.

Finally the effects of varying the intensity of the reaction signal itself have been studied in another investigation (Baumeister *et al.*, 1964). Here it was apparent that the visual reaction times of subnormal subjects improved with an increase in the intensity of the reaction signal although the effect was not pronounced. In contrast, normal subjects were unaffected by variations in intensity of the reaction signal.

Distraction studies

Subnormal patients have been frequently described as abnormally distractible. In their work on figure-ground impairment Werner and his associates (see chapter 4) stressed the hyper-distractibility of some severely subnormal children. We have already considered the work of Schulman and his colleagues (Schulman *et al.*, 1965; see chapter 4) who found that distractibility measures provided the most reliable behavioural indices of some severely retarded brain-damaged children. However, such findings on distractibility are all directly related to the child whose retardation is thought to be a result of brain injury, as distinct from the familial defective child. As the criterion of brain damage adopted in such studies is often an I.Q. below a certain level, it is not altogether clear whether distractibility is a feature associated with brain damage or with subnormality of intelligence.

Most recent work, attempting to examine the figure-background syndrome in subnormals, yields ambiguous results. Cobrinck (1959) studied the effects of intelligence level on the performance of normal and brain-injured children on an embedded figures test. His results showed that while the normal children were significantly superior in performance to the brain-injured children, I.Q. was unrelated to the performance of either group. This conclusion has been questioned in a later investigation (Rosenberg, 1961).

An attempt to clarify this question was made in a study by Cruse (1961) who used groups of familial and brain-damaged subnormal subjects matched for both chronological and mental age. The brain-damaged subnormals were further sub-divided into the two groups of 'indeterminate' and 'determinate' brain damage, the latter group containing those patients whose diagnosis was unequivocal. Reaction-time responses to a visual signal were assessed in distracting and non-distracting conditions. Other variables included in the investigation were the presence and absence of an auditory warning signal and the length of the preparatory interval. Vigilance behaviour was also examined in longer reaction time trials without warning signals. Cruse's analysis demonstrated that there were significant differences in reaction time, vigilance performance, and in the effect of distraction between the familial and determinate brain-damaged defectives, although these differences disappeared if the scores of the indeterminate group were included in the analysis. Somewhat similar results have been reported in another study by Bensberg and Canter (1957) who concluded that brain damage exerts a variable effect on reaction time depending upon the cerebral location of the damage.

The effects of distracting conditions on the learning of subnormals has been investigated in another study (Ellis *et al.*, 1963) with more ambiguous results. Contrary to expectations, the effect of different forms of distraction on normal subjects was to *improve* performance, while distraction was found to have little effect upon the performance of subnormal subjects.

A more careful examination of some of the variables operative in distraction conditions has been conducted by Brown and Clark (1963) and Brown (1964, 1966) in a series of studies of subnormal performance. The initial study of this series (Brown and Clarke, 1963) investigated the effect of both meaningful and meaningless auditory distraction on the object-naming performance of subnormal and severely subnormal groups. It was found that, although both groups were affected by distraction, the severely subnormal group was much more affected by meaningful distraction. However, the form of the meaningful distraction used in this experiment (repetition of the correct object names in the wrong order) may have made this condition particularly confusing to the severely subnormal patients.

In a later study (Brown, 1964) concerned with the effects of visual distraction, attempts were made to discriminate factors which might influence the heterogeneity of attentional behaviour in subnormal subjects. The test involved the reproduction of briefly presented visual figures of varying complexity with and without a distracting surround of thirty-seven background figures. As only half of the subjects tested returned scores showing an adverse effect of distraction it was again evident that distractibility could not be considered as a general factor in subnormality. When samples of the two extremes of intelligence (twelve highest and twelve lowest I.Q. subjects) were compared, no differences were found in distractibility scores, although the least intelligent subjects were inferior in their reproduction of the figures without distraction. When subjects were divided into two groups on the basis of the presence or absence of brain damage (epilepsy, encephalitis, etc.) and their distractibility scores compared, no clear differences were evident. Brown found a tendency for subjects who had been institutionalized early in life to be more distractible than those institutionalized at a later age. The absence of sufficiently detailed information on early pre-institutionalized environment of the subjects obviated any clear examination of the effects of favourable and unfavourable home conditions on later distractibility.

Work outside the clinical field (Pollock and Bartlett, 1932) has confirmed that although normal subjects tend to show a performance decrement in the face of distraction, such effects are transient. In a more recent study Brown (1966) attempted to investigate any differences in the adaptation rates of subnormal subjects to distraction. He used a word fluency task requiring subjects to name as many animals as possible in a thirty-second period. The distracting stimuli consisted of names of tools presented in rapid succession through a tape-recorder at a fairly intense auditory level. Brown's analysis indicated that, although distraction markedly affected the initial performance of the subnormal group most subjects learned to adapt to the extraneous stimulation so that with repeated trials the influence of distraction was lessened until there was no observable decrement in performance. Correlations between intelligence levels and distraction scores showed a tendency for these subjects with a higher I.Q. (subnormals) to adapt more easily than those of a lower I.Q. (severely subnormal). This is in line with the Zeaman-House (1963) hypothesis that severely subnormal subjects take longer to become familiar with the task situation and to discriminate between the relevant and irrelevant cues. As before, Brown was able to demonstrate a non-significant tendency for subjects from poor home environments and subjects institutionalized before the age of nine years to be more distractible. In discussing the practical application of such experimental findings to the education and training of subnormals, Brown (1966) suggests that the training environment should be either distraction-free or at least avoid the presence of discontinuous extraneous stimulation which would prevent adaptation and have greater distraction potential.

Vigilance performance

Vigilance tasks are normally conducted in an environment where all extraneous stimulation is greatly reduced or otherwise controlled and it might therefore be expected that vigilance studies would throw further light on the attentional behaviour of subnormal subjects. Unfortunately, the literature contains few reports of research in this field with intellectually retarded subjects.

Ware, Barker and Sipowicz (1962) examined the vigilance performance of a group of subnormal adults on a task requiring the detection of irregular periodic interruptions (twenty-four signals per hour), or a continuous light source. Subjects monitored the light in an isolated room wearing earphones to reduce extraneous auditory stimulation. Although they reported no significant differences in vigilance performance between subnormal and normal groups, the fact that the normal data were obtained from a separate investigation somewhat reduces the reliability of their results. Semmel (1963) has presented a model of subnormality in which the main factor affecting performance is a deficiency in arousal level. He has subsequently investigated the vigilance behaviour of subnormal subjects, arguing that vigilance decrements are an indirect measure of decaying arousal (Frankman and Adams, 1962). In one of his studies Semmel (1965) reports a comparison of normal and subnormal (I.Q. range 50–75) groups on a one-hour visual vigilance task under controlled environmental conditions. The task required the subjects to detect and respond by key-pressing brief interruptions of a faintly illuminated light bulb. The task was conducted in a uniform non-stimulating visual environment and extraneous auditory stimulation was masked by a constant source of white noise. Under pre-test and post-test alerting conditions where the experimenter gave a verbal warning prior to the presentation of the signal, there were no significant detection differences between the normal and subnormal groups. However, in the non-alerted main vigilance task the performance of the subnormal group was markedly inferior. Comparing different periods of the vigilance watch, it was also evident that the subnormal subjects showed an earlier and more rapid decrement in performance to that demonstrated in the normal subjects. These findings are illustrated in Figure 31

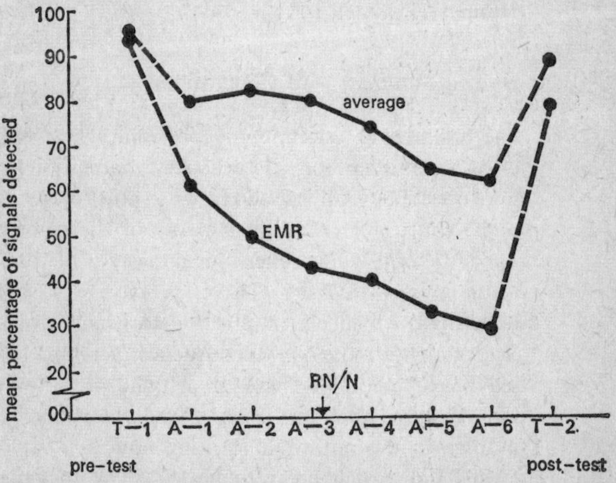

Figure 31 Mean percentage detection scores for the two groups as a function of time spent on the task

which charts the mean percentage detection scores for the two groups as a function of time spent on the task.

The length of the interval between signals was found to affect vigilance performance, errors being more common where signals were separated by a relatively long interval.

However, this effect was equally observable in both groups of subjects and therefore did not appear to be a function of intelligence. Semmel (1965) interprets these findings to suggest that, under environmental conditions of reduced sensory variation, subnormal subjects experience a more rapid decay in alertness or arousal than subjects of normal intelligence. Normal subjects only begin to show a marked decrement in performance after about forty minutes, whereas subnormal subjects show a marked loss in vigilance efficiency in only half this time. Semmel concludes that 'The old dictum "dull minds for dull jobs" is not supported by the results of this experiment. On the contrary, retarded children, when compared to their average peers, apparently suffer more from dull, monotonous environments where the maintenance of alert behaviour is required' (Semmel, 1965).

General Summary and Conclusions

The attempt to examine the possibility that subnormal individuals suffer from disturbances of attention has raised more questions than it has so far been able to answer. Much of the confusion and a great many of the contradictions reflect the highly heterogeneous nature of this broad diagnostic group. In particular, it is extremely difficult to disentangle which effects are due to brain damage from those which are the sole consequence of retarded intellectual development. The heterogeneity in subnormal populations suggests that the practical significance of research findings to the optimum learning environment for subnormal individuals are very limited. The fact that many subnormal individuals are subjected to a great deal of early emotional and social deprivation emphasizes the need to consider the role of motivational factors in all attentional studies.

A Concluding Comment

This review of studies concerned with disturbances of attention in psychiatric patients permits few firm conclusions. Most of the reported findings are open to a variety of interpretations and a great deal more work will be necessary before their significance is fully assessed. Perhaps the most encouraging sign is the continual attempt to examine abnormal behaviour within a discipline of scientific methodology. Only a decade ago many of the aspects of disturbed behaviour which are now being examined were considered to be too subjective to lend themselves to experimental inquiry. The patient unravelling of the many complex variables involved in attentional deficits is already leading to a more reliable and precise identification of the basic mechanisms involved. Later volumes in this series will show that a similar position is being reached in the case of other cognitive processes such as remembering and thinking. Although the affective and conative components of behaviour present a more difficult problem for objective investigation, the application of new techniques to the study of emotional and motivational changes has already suggested how such problems may be overcome.

Many years ago Freud suggested that any analysis of disturbed behaviour must also throw some light on the processes involved in normal behaviour. In recent years clinical psychology has gained enormously from the expertise and basic methodology of the experimental investigator in the normal field. Perhaps this debt may soon be repaid as the significance of clinical studies to normal mental processes becomes increasingly apparent.

References

Ackner, B., and Pampiglione, G. (1959), 'An evaluation of the sedation threshold test', *Journal of Psychosomatic Research*, vol. 3, pp. 271–81.

Bannister, D. (1962), 'The nature and measurement of schizophenic thought disorder', *Journal of Mental Science*, vol. 108, pp. 825–42.

Bateson, G., Jackson, D. D., Haley, J., and Weakland, J. H. (1956), 'Toward a theory of schizophrenia', *Behavioral Science*, vol. 1, pp. 251–64.

Baumeister, A., and Ellis, N. R. (1963), 'Delayed response performance of retardates', *American Journal of Mental Deficiency*, vol. 67, pp. 714–22.

Baumeister, A., Hawkins, W. F., and Kellas, T. (1965), 'The inter-active effects of stimulus intensity upon reaction time', *American Journal of Mental Deficiency*, vol. 69, pp. 526–30.

Baumeister, A., Hawkins, W. F., and Koenigsknecht, R. (1965), 'Effects of variations of complexity of the warning signal upon reaction time', *American Journal of Mental Deficiency*, vol. 69, pp. 860–66.

Baumeister, A., Urquart, D., Beedle, R., and Smith, D. E. (1964), 'Reaction times of subnormals and retardates under different stimulus intensities', *American Journal of Mental Deficiency*, vol. 69, pp. 126–30.

Bensberg, G. J., and Cantor, G. N. (1957), 'Reaction time in mental defectives with organic and familial aetiology', *American Journal of Mental Deficiency*, vol. 62, pp. 534–7.

Benton, A. L., and Joynt, R. (1959), 'Reaction time in

unilateral cerebral disease', *Confinia Neurologica*, vol. 19, pp. 247–56.

Berlyne, D. E. (1960), *Conflict, Arousal and Curiosity*, McGraw-Hill.

Birch, H. G., Belmont, L., and Karp, E. (1964), 'Excitation-inhibition balance in brain-damaged patients', *Journal of Nervous and Mental Diseases*, vol. 139, pp. 537–44.

Birch, H. G., Belmont, L., and Karp, E. (1965), 'The prolongation of inhibition in brain-damaged patients', *Cortex*, vol. 1, no. 4, pp. 397–409.

Birch, H. G., Belmont, L., and Karp, E. (1967), 'Delayed processing and extinction', *Brain*, vol. 90, pp. 113–24.

Birren, J., and Bottwinck, J. (1955), 'Speed of response as a function of perceptual difficulty and age', *Journal of Gerontology*, vol. 10, pp. 433–6.

Blackburn, H. L., and Benton, A. L. (1955), 'Simple and choice reaction time in cerebral disease', *Confinia Neurologica*, vol. 15, pp. 327–8.

Bleuler, E. (1911), *Dementia Praecox of the Group of Schizophrenias*, International Universities Press, 1950.

Bowers, M. V., and Freedman, D. (1966), 'Psychedelic experiences in acute psychoses', *Archives of General Psychiatry*, vol. 15, pp. 240–48.

Brain, R. (1958), 'The physiological basis of consciousness', *Brain*, vol. 81, 426–55.

Broadbent, D. E. (1954), 'Role of auditory localisation and attention in memory span', *Journal of Experimental Psychology*, vol. 47, pp. 191–6.

Broadbent, D. E. (1958), *Perception and Communication*, Pergamon Press.

Broadbent, D. E., and Gregory, M. (1963), 'Vigilance considered as statistical decision', *British Journal of Psychology*, vol. 54, pp. 309–23.

Broadbent, D. E., and Heron, A. (1962), 'The effects of a subsidiary task on performance involving immediate memory by younger and older men', *British Journal of Psychology*, vol. 53, pp. 189–98.

Brown, G. W. (1960), 'Length of hospital stay in schizophrenia: A review of statistical studies', *Acta Psychiatrica et Neurologica Scandinavica*, vol. 35, pp. 414–30.

Brown, R. I. (1964), The effects of visual distraction on perception in subjects of sub-normal intelligence', *British Journal of Social and Clinical Psychology*, vol. 1, pp. 20–8.

Brown, R. I. (1966), 'The effects of extraneous auditory stimulation on learning and performance', *American Journal of Mental Deficiency*, vol. 71, pp. 283–91.

Brown, R. I., and Clarke, A. D. B. (1963), 'The effects of auditory distraction on institutionalised sub-normal and severely sub-normal subjects', *Gib. Ment. Def.*, Press 7, 1, pp. 1–190.

Bruner, J. S. (1957), 'On perceptual readiness', *Psychological Review*, vol. 64, pp. 123–33.

Bryant, A. R. P. (1961), *An Investigation of Process-reaction Schizophrenia with Relation to Perception of Visual Space*, Unpublished Doctoral Thesis, University of Utah.

Bzhalava, I. T. (1965), 'On the psychopathology of fixated set in epilepsy and schizophrenia', *Cortex*, vol. 1, no. 4, pp. 493–507.

Cameron, N. (1938), 'Reasoning, regression and communication in schizophrenics', *Psychological Monographs*, vol. 50, no. 221, pp. 1–34.

Cameron, N. (1939), 'Deterioration and regression in schizophrenic thinking', *Journal of Abnormal Social Psychology*, vol. 34, pp. 265–70.

Cameron, N. (1951), 'Perceptual organisation and behaviour pathology', in R. R. Blake and G. V. Ramsey (eds.), *Perception: An Approach to Personality*, Ronald Press, New York.

Cameron, N., and Magaret, A. (1949), 'Experimental studies in thinking. 1. Scattered speech in the responses of normal subjects to incomplete sentences', *Journal of Experimental Psychology*, vol. 39, pp. 617–27.

Cameron, N., and Magaret, A .(1950), 'Correlates of scattered speech in the responses of normal subjects to incomplete sentences', *Journal of General Psychology*, vol. 43, pp. 77–84.

Campbell, R. J., and Harlow, H. F. (1945), 'Problem solution by monkeys following bilateral removal of the prefrontal areas. 5. Special delayed reactions', *Journal of Experimental Psychology*, vol. 35, pp. 110–26.

Chapman, L. J. (1956), 'Distractibility in the conceptual performance of schizophrenics', *Journal of Abnormal and Social Psychology*, vol. 53, pp. 286–91.

Chapman, J., and McGhie, A. (1962), 'A comparative study of disordered attention of schizophrenia', *Journal of Mental Science*, vol. 108, pp. 487–500.

Chapman, J., and McGhie, A. (1963), 'An approach to the psychotherapy of cognitive dysfunction in schizophrenia', *British Journal of Medical Psychology*, vol. 34, pp. 253–60.

Chapman, L. J., and Taylor, J. A. (1957), 'Breadth of deviate concepts used by schizophrenics', *Journal of Abnormal and Social Psychology*, vol. 54, pp. 118–23.

Cherry, E. C. (1953), 'On the recognition of speech with one and with two ears', *Journal of the Acoustical Society of America*, vol. 25, pp. 975–9.

Claridge, G. S. (1969), 'The excitation-inhibition balance in neurotics', in H. J. Eysenck (ed.), *Experiments in Personality*, Routledge and Kegan Paul.

Claridge, G. S. (1967), *Personality and Arousal. A Psychophysiological Study of Psychiatric Disorder*, Pergamon Press.

Claridge, G. G., and Herrington, R. N. (1963a), 'Excitation-inhibition and the theory of neuroses. A study of the sedation threshold', in H. J. Eysenck (ed.), *Experiments with Drugs*, Pergamon Press.

Claridge, G. S., and Herrington, R. N. (1963b), 'An E.E.G. correlate of the Archimedes spiral after-effect and its relationship with personality', *Behaviour, Research and Therapy*, vol. 1, pp. 217–29.

Clements, S. D. (1966), 'Minimal brain dysfunctions in children – identification and terminology', *Public Health Service Publication*, no. 1415.

Cobrinck, L. (1959), 'The performance of brain-injured children on hidden-figure tests', *American Journal of Psychology*, vol. 72, pp. 566–71.

Cohen, L. H., and Patterson, M. (1937), 'The effect of pain on the heart rate of normal and schizophrenic individuals', *Journal of General Psychology*, vol. 17, pp. 273–9.

Conrad, R. (1964), 'Acoustic confusions in immediate memory', *British Journal of Psychology*, vol. 55, p. 75.

Corsellis, J. A. N. (1962), 'Mental illness and the ageing brain', *Maudsley Hospital Monograph*, no. 9, Oxford University Press.

Costa, L. D. (1962), 'Visual reaction time of patients with cerebral disease as a function of length and constancy of preparatory interval', *Perceptual and Motor Skills*, vol. 14, pp. 391–7.

Costello, C. G. (1956), 'The effects of pre-frontal leucotomy upon visual imagery and the ability to perform complex operations', *Journal of Mental Science*, vol. 428, pp. 507–16.

Cromwell, R., Rosenthal, D., Shakow, D., and Zahn, T. (1961), 'Reaction time, locus of control, choice behaviour and descriptions of parental behaviour in schizophrenic and normal subjects', *Journal of Personality*, vol. 29, pp. 363–79.

Crookes, T. G. (1957), 'Size constancy and literalness in schizophrenia', *British Journal of Medical Psychology*, vol. 30, pp. 99–106.

Cruse, D. B. (1961), 'The effects of distraction on the performance of brain-injured and familial retarded children', *American Journal of Mental Deficiency*, vol. 66, pp. 86–93.

Darrow, C. W., Pathman, J., and Kronenberg, G. (1946), 'Level of autonomic activity and electroencephalogram', *Journal of Experimental Psychology*, vol. 36, pp. 355–65.

Davis, P. A., and Davis, H. (1939), 'The electroencephalograms of psychotic patients', *American Journal of Psychiatry*, vol. 95. pp. 1007–25.

Davis, R. (1956), 'The limits of the psychological refractory period', *Quarterly Journal of Experimental Psychology*, vol. 8, pp. 24–31.

De Renzi, E., and Faglioni, P. (1965), 'The comparative efficiency of intelligence and vigilance tests in detecting hemispheric cerebral damage', *Cortex*, vol. 1, no. 4, pp. 410–18.

Deutsch, J. A., and Deutsch, D. (1963), 'Attention: some theoretical considerations', *Psychological Review*, vol. 70, pp. 5–15.

Deutsch, C. P., and Zawel, D. (1966), 'Comparison of visual and auditory perceptual functions of brain-injured and normal children', *Perceptual and Motor Skills*, vol. 22, pp. 303–9.

Efstathiou, A., and Morant, R. B. (1966), 'Persistence of the waterfall illusion after-effect as a test of brain damage', *Journal of Abnormal Psychology*, vol. 71, pp. 300–3.

Eitinger, L., Laane, C. J., and Langfeldt, G. (1958), 'The prognostic value of the clinical picture and the therapeutic value of physical treatment in schizophrenia and the schizophreniform states', *Acta Psychiatrica Neurologica*, vol. 33, pp. 33–41.

Ellis, N. R. (1963), 'A stimulus trace and behavioural inadequacy', in M. R. Ellis (ed.), *Handbook of Mental Deficiency*, McGraw-Hill.

Ellis, N. R., Hawkins, W. F., Pryer, N. W., and Jones, R. W. (1963), 'Distraction effects in auditory learning by normal and mentally defective humans', *American Journal of Mental Deficiency*, vol. 67, p. 576.

English Division of Professional Psychologists (Educational and Clinical) (1963), 'Report of the working party on sub-normality', *Bulletin of the British Psychological Society*, vol. 16, no. 53, pp. 37–40.

Eysenck, H. J. (1947), *Dimensions of Personality*, Kegan Paul.

Eysenck, H. J., Granger, G. W., and Brengelmann, J. C. (1957), 'Perceptual processes in mental illness', *Maudsley Hospital Monograph*, no. 2.

Feinberg, I., and Mercer, M. (1960), 'Studies of thought disorder in schizophrenia', *American Medical Association Archives of General Psychiatry*, vol. 2, pp. 504–13.

Fleishman, E. A. (1954), 'Dimensional analysis of psychomotor abilities', *Journal of Experimental Psychology*, vol. 48, pp. 437–54.

Foulds, G. A. (1951), 'Temperamental differences in maze performance. Part 1. Characteristics differences among psycho-neurotics', *British Journal of Psychology*, vol. 42, pp. 209–21.

Frankmann, J. P., and Adams, J. A. (1962), 'Theories of vigilance', *Psychological Bulletin*, vol. 59, pp. 257–74.

Freeman, T., Cameron, J. L., and McGhie, A. (1958), *Chronic Schizophrenia*, Tavistock Publications.

Freeman, T., Cameron, J. L., and McGhie, A. (1966), *Studies on Psychoses*, Tavistock Publications.

French, J. D., Hernández-Peón, R., and Livingston, R. B. (1955), 'Projections from cortex to cephalic brain stem (reticular formation) in monkeys', *Journal of Neurophysiology*, vol. 18, pp. 74–95.

Freud, S. (1920), *Beyond the Pleasure Principle*, Standard Edition, vol. 18, Hogarth Press, 1955.

Friedman, A. S. (1964), 'Minimal effects of severe depression on cognitive functioning', *Journal of Abnormal and Social Psychology*, vol. 69, pp. 237–41.

Fulcher, J. H., Gallacher, W. H., and Pfeiffer, C. C. (1957), 'Comparative lucid intervals after amobarbitol, CO_2 and Arecoline in chronic schizophrenics', *American Medical Association Archives of Neurological Psychiatry*, vol. 78, pp. 392–8.

Fulton, J. F. (1949), *Physiology of the Nervous System*, Oxford University Press.

Galambos, R. (1956), 'Suppression of auditory nerve activity by stimulation of efferent fibres to cochlea', *Journal of Neurophysiology*, vol. 19, pp. 424–37.

Gardner, R. W. (1961), 'Field articulation in recall', *Psychological Record*, vol. 11, pp. 305–21.

Gardner, R. W., Holzman, P. S., Klein, G. S., Linton, H. B., and Spence, D. P. (1959), 'Cognitive control: A study of individual consistencies in cognitive behaviour', *Psychological Issues*, vol. 1, no. 4.

Goldberg, L. R., and Smith, P. A. (1958), 'The clinical usefulness of the Archimedes spiral in the diagnosis of organic brain damage', *Journal of Consulting Psychology*, vol. 22, pp. 253–62.

Goldman-Eisler, F. (1961), 'The distribution of pause durations in speech', *Language and Speech*, vol. 4, pp. 232–7.

Goldstein, K. (1927), 'Die Lokalisation in der Grosshirnrinde', in A. Bethe and E. Fisher (eds.), *Handbuch der Normale und Pathologischen Physiologie*, Springer, Berlin.

Goldstein, K. (1939), *The Organism*, New York American Book Company.

Goldstein, K. (1944), 'Methodological approach to the study of schizophrenic thought disorder', in J. S. Kasanin (ed.), *Language and Thought in Schizophrenia*, University of California Press.

Goldstein, K., and Sheerer, M. (1941), 'Abstract and concrete behaviour: an experimental study with special tests', *Psychological Monographs*, vol. 53, no. 239.

Goldstein, L., Murphe, H. B., Sugarmann, A. A., Pfeiffer, C. C., and Jenney, E. H. (1963), 'Quantitative electroencephalographic analysis of naturally occurring schizophrenia and drug induced psychotic states in human males', *Clinical Pharmacology and Therapeutics*, vol. 4, pp. 10–15.

Goldstein, L., Sugarmann, A. A., Stolberg, H., Murphe, H. B., and Pfeiffer, C. C. (1965), 'Electro-cerebral activity in schizophrenics and non-psychotic subjects: Quantitative E.E.G. amplitude analysis', *Electroence-*

phalography and Clinical Neurophysiology, vol. 19, pp. 350–60.

Granit, R. (1955), 'Centrifugal and antidromic effects on ganglion cells of retina', *Journal of Neurophysiology*, vol. 18, pp. 388–98.

Griew, S., and Davies, D. R. (1962), 'The effect of ageing on auditory vigilance performance', *Journal of Gerontology*, vol. 17, pp. 88–90.

Hamilton, V. (1963), 'Size constancy and cue responsiveness in psychoses', *British Journal of Psychology*, vol. 54, pp. 25–39.

Harris, J. G. (1957), 'Size estimation of pictures as a function of thematic content for schizophrenic and normal subjects', *Journal of Personality*, vol. 25, pp. 651–71.

Hassol, L., Magaret, A., and Cameron, N. (1952), 'The production of language disorganisation through personalized distraction', *Journal of Psychology*, vol. 35, pp. 289–97.

Hawkins, W. F., Baumeister, A. A., and Holland, J. M. (1965), 'Reaction time in retardates following variations in the warning signal intensity and preparatory interval', *American Journal of Mental Deficiency*, vol. 70, pp. 135–8.

Hebb, D. O. (1955), *The Organisation of Behaviour*, Chapman and Hall.

Hecker, E. (1871), 'Die Hebephrenia', *Virchows Archiv für pathologische Anatomie und Physiologie und für klinische Medizin*, vol. 71, pp. 52–394.

Henderson, D., and Gillespie, R. D. (1962), *Textbook of Psychiatry*, 9th edition, revised by D. Henderson and I. R. C. Batchelor, Oxford University Press.

Herrington, R. N., and Claridge, G. S. (1965), 'Sedation threshold and Archimedes spiral effect in early psychoses', *Journal of Psychiatric Research*, vol. 3, pp. 159–70.

Hick, W. E. (1952), 'The rate of gain of information', *Quarterly Journal of Experimental Psychology*, vol. 4, pp. 11–26.

Holland, H. C. (1965), *The Spiral After-Effect*, Pergamon Press.

Holland, H. C., and Beech, H. R. (1958), 'The spiral after-effect as a test of brain damage', *Journal of Mental Science*, vol. 104, pp. 446–71.

Hume, W. I., and Claridge, G. S. (1965), 'A comparison of two measures of arousal in normal subjects', *Life Sciences*, vol. 4, pp. 545–53.

Hunt, J. McV., and Cofer, C. N. (1944), 'Physiological deficit', in J. McV. Hunt (ed.), *Personality and Behaviour Disorders*, vol. 2, Ronald Press, New York.

Huston, P. E., Cohen, B. D., and Senf, R. (1955), 'Shifting of set and goal orientation in schizophrenia', *Journal of Mental Science*, vol. 101, pp. 344–50.

Huston, P. E., and Shakow, D. (1948), 'Learning in schizophrenia: 1. Pursuit learning', *Journal of Personality*, vol. 17, pp. 52–74.

Huston, P. E., and Shakow, D. (1949), 'Learning capacity in schizophrenia; with special reference to the concept of deterioration', *American Journal of Psychiatry*, vol. 105, pp. 881–8.

Huston, P. C., Shakow, D., and Riggs, L. A. (1937), 'Studies of motor function in schizophrenia: II. Reaction time', *Journal of General Psychology*, vol. 16, pp. 39–82.

Hyman, R. (1953), 'Stimulus information as a determinant of reaction time', *Journal of Experimental Psychology*, vol. 45, pp. 188–96.

Kahlbaum, K. (1874), *Katatonie oder das Spannungsirresein; Klinische Abhandlungen über Psychische Krankheiten*, Heft, Berlin.

Kay, D. W. K., Beamish, P., and Roth, M. (1964), 'Old age mental disorders in Newcastle-upon Tyne: Part 1', *British Journal of Psychiatry*, vol. 110, pp. 146–58.

Khomskaya, Y. D. (1965), 'The verbal regulation of vegetative components of the orienting reflex in patients with differently located brain lesions', *Voprosy Psikhologii*, vol. 2, no. 1, pp. 55–66.

Kimura, D. (1961), 'Some effects of temporal lobe damage on auditory perception', *Canadian Journal of Psychology*, vol. 15, pp. 156–65.

Kimura, D. (1964), 'Cognitive deficit related to seizure pattern in centrencephalic epilepsy', *Journal of Neurology, Neurosurgery and Psychiatry*, vol. 27, pp. 291–5.

Kimura, D. (1966), 'Dual functional asymmetry of the brain and visual perception', *Neuropsychologica*, vol. 4, pp. 275–85.

Kind, H. (1966), 'The psychogenesis of schizophrenia; a review of the literature', *British Journal of Psychiatry*, vol. 112, pp. 333–50.

King, H. E. (1954), *Psychomotor Aspects of Mental Disease*, Commonwealth Fund, Harvard University Press.

Knehr, C. A. (1954), 'Schizophrenic reaction time responses to variable preparatory intervals', *American Journal of Psychiatry*, vol. 110, pp. 585–8.

Kornetsky, C., and Mirsky, A. F. (1966), 'On certain psychopharmacological and physiological differences between schizophrenic and normal persons', *Psychopharmacologia*, vol. 8, pp. 309–17.

Kraepelin, E. (1896), *Lehrbuch der Psychiatrie*, Barth, Leipzig.

Krishnamoorti, S. R., and Shagass, C. (1964), 'Some psychological test correlates of sedation threshold', in J. Wartis (ed.), *Recent Advances in Biological Psychiatry*, vol. 6, Plenum, New York.

Kubie, L. F. (1954), 'Psychiatric and psycho-analytic considerations of the problems of consciousness', in J. F. Delafresnaye (ed.), *Brain Mechanisms and Consciousness*, Blackwell Scientific Publications, Oxford.

Laffal, J. (1961), 'Changes in the language of a schizophrenic patient during psychotherapy', *Journal of Abnormal and Social Psychology*, vol. 63.

Landsell, H., and Mirsky, A. F. (1964), 'Attention in focal and centrencephalic epilepsy, *Experimental Neurology*, vol. 9, pp. 463–80.

Langfeldt, G. (1939), *The Schizophreniform States*, Munksgaard, Copenhagen.

Lawson, J. S. (1965), *Disorders of Attention and Language in Schizophrenia*, Unpublished Ph.D. Thesis, University of St Andrews.

Lawson, J. S., McGhie, A., and Chapman, J. (1964), 'Perception of speech in schizophrenia', *British Journal of Psychiatry*, vol. 110, pp. 375–83.

Lawson, J. S., McGhie, A., and Chapman, J. (1967), 'Distractibility in schizophrenic and organic cerebral disease', *British Journal of Psychiatry*, vol. 113, pp. 527–35.

Lehmann, N. (1966), 'Pharmacotherapy of schizophrenia', in P. Hoch and J. Zubin (eds.), *Psychopathology of Schizophrenia*, Grune and Stratton.

Leonhard, H. (1959), *Die Aufteilung der Endogenon Psychosen*, Berlin Akademie Verlag.

Lewis, A. (1935), 'Problems of obsessional illness', *Proceedings of the Royal Society of Medicine*, vol. 29, pp. 325–30.

Lindsley, D. B. (1958), 'The reticular formation and perceptual discrimination in H. H. Jasper *et al.* (eds.), *Reticular Formation of the Brain*, Churchill.

Lindsley, D. B. (1960), 'Attention, consciousness, sleep and wakefulness', in J. Field (ed.), *Handbook of Physiology. Section 1: Neurophysiology*, American Physiological Society, Washington, p. 1553.

Lovinger, E. (1956), 'Perceptual contact with reality in schizophrenia', *Journal of Abnormal and Social Psychology*, vol. 52, pp. 87–91.

Lowe, G. R. (1966), 'Response inhibition and deviant social behaviour in children', *British Journal of Psychiatry*, vol. 112, pp. 929–30.

Luria, A. R. (1960), 'Verbal regulational behaviour', in M. A. B. Brazier (ed.), *The Central Nervous System and Behaviour, Transactions of the Third Conference*, Josiah Macey Jr Foundation, New York.

Luria, A. R. (1961), in J. Tizard (ed.), *The Role of Speech in the Regulation of Normal and Abnormal Behaviour*, Liveright Publ. Corp., New York.

Luria, A. R. (1963), 'Psychological studies of mental deficiency in the Soviet Union', in N. R. Ellis (ed.), *Handbook of Mental Deficiency*, McGraw-Hill.

Luria, A. R., Homskaya, A. A., Blinkov, S. M., and Critchley, M. (1967), 'Impaired selectivity in mental processes in association with a lesion of the frontal lobe', *Neuropsychologia*, vol. 5, pp. 105–23.

Lynn, R. (1966), *Attention, Arousal and the Orientation Reaction*, Pergamon Press.

McDonald, N. (1960), 'Living with schizophrenia', *Canadian Medical Association Journal*, vol. 82, pp. 218–27.

McDonald, R. D., and Burns, S. B. (1964), 'Visual vigilance and brain damage. An empirical study', *Journal of Neurology, Neurosurgery and Psychiatry*, vol. 27, pp. 206–9.

McGhie, A., and Chapman, J. (1961), 'Disorders of attention and perception in early schizophrenia', *British Journal of Medical Psychology*, vol. 34, pp. 103–16.

McGhie, A., Chapman, J., and Lawson, J. S. (1964), 'Disturbances in selective attention in schizophrenia', *Proceedings of the Royal Society of Medicine*, vol. 57, pp. 419–22.

McGhie, A., Chapman, J., and Lawson, J. S. (1965), 'Changes in immediate memory with age', *British Journal of Psychology*, vol. 56, pp. 69–75.

McGhie, A., Chapman, J., and Lawson, J. S. (1965a), 'The effect of distraction on schizophrenic performance: 1. Psychomotor ability', *British Journal of Psychiatry*, vol. 111, pp. 391–8.

McGhie, A., Chapman J. and Lawson, J. S. (1965b), The effect of distraction on schizophrenic performance: 2. Perception and immediate memory', *British Journal of Psychiatry*, vol. 111, pp. 383–90.

McKerracher, B. W., and Scott, J. (1966), 'I.Q. scores and

problem of classification', *British Journal of Psychiatry*, vol. 112, pp. 537–42.

Maher, B. A. (1966), *Principles of Psychopathology*, McGraw-Hill.

Maher, B. A., Elder, S. T., and Noblin, C. D. (1962), 'A differential investigation of avoidance reduction versus hypermotility following frontal ablation', *Journal of Comparative and Physiological Psychology*, vol. 55, pp. 449–54.

Malmo, R. B. (1957), 'Anxiety and behavioural arousal', *Psychological Review*, vol. 64, pp. 276–87.

Malmo, R. B., Shagass, C., and David, F. H. (1951), 'Electromyographic studies of muscular tension in psychiatric patients under stress', *Journal of Clinical and Experimental Psychopathology*, vol. 12, pp. 45–66.

Meldman, M. J. (1964a), 'P.R.R. study 2: Verification of hyperattentionism in phobic reaction', *American Journal of Psychiatry*, vol. 121, no. 1, pp. 70–71.

Meldman, M. J. (1964b), 'A nosology of the attentional diseases', *American Journal of Psychiatry*, vol. 121, no. 4, pp. 377–8.

Meldman, M. J. (1965), 'The quantitative analysis of anxiety and depression', *Psychosomatics*, vol. 6, no. 1, pp. 8–11.

Meyer, A. (1906), 'Fundamental conceptions of dementia praecox', *British Medical Journal*, vol. 2, pp. 757–64.

Meyer, A. (1910), 'The dynamic interpretation of dementia praecox', *American Journal of Psychology*, vol. 21, pp. 385–92.

Meyer, V., (1957), 'Critique of psychological approaches to brain damage', *Journal of Mental Science*, vol. 103, pp. 80–95.

Meyer, V. (1961), 'Psychological effects of brain damage', in H. J. Eysenck (ed.), *Handbook of Abnormal Psychology*, Basic Books.

Miller, G. A. (1963), 'Decision units in the perception of speech', *Institute of Radio Engineers Transactions on Information Theory*, It-8, 81.

Miller, G. A., and Selfridge, J. A. (1950), 'Verbal content and the recall of meaningful material', *American Journal of Psychology*, vol. 63, pp. 176–83.

Milner, B. (1958), 'Psychological defects produced by temporal lobe excision', *Proceedings of the Association of Research into Nervous and Mental Diseases*, vol. 36, pp. 244–57.

Milner, B., and Penfield, W. (1965), 'The effect of hippocampal lesions on recent memory', *Transactions of the American Neurological Association*, vol. 80, pp. 42–8.

Mirsky, A. F., Primac, D. W., Ajmone Marsan, C., Rosvold, H. E., and Stevens, J. R. (1960), 'A comparison of patients with focal and non-focal epilepsy on a test of attention', *Experimental Neurology*, vol. 2, pp. 75–89.

Morant, R. B., and Efstathiou, A. (1966), 'The Archimedes spiral and diagnosis of brain damage', *Perceptual and Motor Skills*, vol. 22, pp. 319–25.

Morel, B. (1860), *Traites de Maladies Mentales*, Masson, Paris.

Morris, J. (1963), 'Analysis of schizophrenic interviews', *British Journal of Medical Psychology*, vol. 36, pp. 283–92.

Obrist, W. D. (1963), 'E.E.G. approach to age changes in response speed', in A. T. Walford and J. E. Birren (eds.), *Behavior, Ageing and the Nervous System*, Charles C. Thomas, Illinois.

O'Connor, N., and Hermelin, B. (1963), *Speech and Thought in Severe Subnormality*, Pergamon Press.

Orzack, M. H., and Kornetsky, C. (1966), 'Attention dysfunction in schizophrenia', *American Medical Association: Archives of General Psychiatry*, vol. 14, pp. 323–6.

Page, H. A., Rakita, G., Kaplan, H. K., and Smith, N. B. (1957), 'Another application of the spiral after-effect in the determination of brain damage', *Journal of Consulting Psychology*, vol. 21, pp. 89–95.

Payne, R. W. (1961), 'Cognitive abnormalities', in H. J.

Eysenck (ed.), *Handbook of Abnormal Psychology*, Basic Books.

Payne, R. W. (1964), *The Measurement and Significance of Overinclusive Thinking and Retardation in Schizophrenic Patients*, paper presented to American Psychopathological Association, 1964.

Payne, R. W., and Caird, W. K. (1967), 'Reactive time, distractibility and overinclusive thinking in psychotics', *Journal of Abnormal Psychology*, vol. 72, pp. 112–21.

Payne, R. W., Caird, W. K., and Laverty, S. G. (1964), 'Overinclusive thinking and delusions in schizophrenic patients', *Journal of Abnormal and Social Psychology*, vol. 68, pp. 562–6.

Payne, R. W., and Hewlett, H. G. (1960), 'Thought disorder in psychotic patients', in H. J. Eysenck (ed.), *Experiments on Personality*, vol. 2, Routledge and Kegan Paul.

Penfield, W. (1954a), 'Studies of the cerebral cortex in man – a view and interpretation', in J. F. Delafresnaye (ed.), *Brain Mechanisms and Consciousness*, Blackwell Scientific Publications.

Penfield, W. (1954b), 'Temporal lobe epilepsy', *British Journal of Surgery*, vol. 41, p. 337.

Phillips, L. (1953), 'Case history data and prognosis in schizophrenia', *Journal of Nervous and Mental Diseases*, vol. 117, pp. 515–25.

Piaget, J. (1961), *Les Mécanismes Perceptifs*, Presses Universitaires de France.

Piercy, M. (1964), 'The effect of cerebral lesions on intellectual functions: A review of current research trends', *British Journal of Psychiatry*, vol. 110, pp. 310–52.

Pollock, K. G., and Bartlett, F. C. (1932), 'Psychological experiments on the effects of noise', *Industrial Health Research Board*, Paper no. 65.

Poppelreuter, W. (1918), *Die Psychischen Schadigung durch Kopfschuss im Kriege, 1914–1917*.

Price, A. C., and Deabler, H. L. (1955), 'Diagnosis of

organicity by means of spiral after-effect', *Journal of Consulting Psychology*, vol. 19, pp. 299–302.

Rabbitt, P. (1963), 'Age and discrimination between complex stimuli', in A. T. Welford and J. E. Birren (eds.), *Behaviour, Ageing and the Nervous System*, Charles C. Thomas, Illinois.

Rabbitt, P., and Birren, J. E. (1967), 'Age and responses to sequences of repetitive and interruptive signals', *Journal of Gerontology*, vol. 22, pp. 143–50.

Raush, H. L. (1952), 'Perceptual constancy in schizophrenia', *Journal of Personality*, vol. 21, pp. 176–87.

Rodnick, E. H., and Shakow, D. (1940), 'Set in the schizophrenic as measured by a composite reaction time index', *American Journal of Psychiatry*, vol. 97, pp. 214–25.

Rosenberg, S. (1961), 'Searching behaviour in the retarded as a function of stimulus exposure conditions and I.Q.', *American Journal of Mental Deficiency*, vol. 65, pp. 749–52.

Rosenthal, D., Lawlor, W. G., Zahn, P. P., and Shakow, D. (1960), 'The relationship of some aspects of mental set to degree of schizophrenic disorganisation', *Journal of Personality*, vol. 28, pp. 26–38.

Rosvold, H. E., Mirsky, A. F., Sarason, I., Bransome, E. D., and Beck, L. H. (1956), 'A continuous performance test of brain damage', *Journal of Consulting Psychology*, vol. 20, pp. 343–52.

Rosvold, H. E., and Mishkin, M. (1961), 'Non-sensory effects of frontal lesions on discrimination learning and performance', in J. Delafresnaye (ed.), *Brain Mechanisms and Learning*, Blackwell Scientific Publications.

Rousseau, J. J. (1857), *De La Folie et L'Epoque de la Puberté*, Thesis, University of Paris.

Russo, M., and Vignolo, L. A. (1967), 'Visual figure-ground discrimination in patients with unilateral disease', *Cortex*, vol. 3, no. 1, pp. 113–21.

Rylander, T. (1939), 'Personality changes after operations on the frontal lobe; A clinical study of 32 cases', *Acta Psychiatrica and Neurologica,* supp. 20.

Samuels, I. (1959), 'Reticular mechanisms and behaviour', *Psychological Bulletin,* vol. 56, pp. 1–12.

Schein, J. D. (1962), 'Cross validation of the continuous performance test for brain damage', *Journal of Consulting Psychology,* vol. 26, pp. 115–21.

Schilder, P. (1951), *Brain and Personality,* New York University Press.

Schlanger, B. B. (1958), 'Results of varying presentation to brain-damaged children of an auditory word discrimination test', *American Journal of Mental Deficiency,* vol. 63, pp. 464–8.

Schulman, J. L., Kasper, J. C., and Throne, F. M. (1965), *Brain Damage and Behaviour: A Clinical-Experimental Study,* Charles C. Thomas, Illinois.

Scott, T. R., Bragg, R. A., and Smarr, R. G. (1963), 'Brain damage diagnosis with the M.M.G.', *Journal of Consulting Psychology,* vol. 27, pp. 45–50.

Semmel, M. I. (1963), *Arousal Theory Applied to Vigilance Behaviour of Educable Mentally Retarded and Average Children,* Unpublished Doctoral Thesis, George Peabody College, Tennessee.

Semmel, M. I. (1965), 'Behaviour of educable retarded and average children', *American Journal of Mental Deficiency,* vol. 70, pp. 38–46.

Shagass, C. (1954), 'The sedation threshold: A method for estimating tension in the psychiatric patient', *E.E.G. and Clinical Neurophysiology,* vol. 6, pp. 221–33.

Shagass, C. (1960), 'Drug thresholds as indicators of personality and affect', in L. Uhr and J. G. Miller (eds.), *Drugs and Behaviour,* Wiley, New York.

Shagass, C. and Jones, A. L. (1958), 'A neurophysiological test for psychiatric diagnosis; results on 750 patients', *American Journal of Psychiatry,* vol. 114, pp. 1002–9.

Shakow, D. (1962), 'Segmental set: A theory of the formal psychological deficit of schizophrenia', *American*

Medical Association, Archives of General Psychiatry, vol. 6, pp. 1–17.

Shakow, D. (1963), 'Psychological deficit in schizophrenia', *Behavioral Science*, vol. 8, pp. 275–305.

Shakow, D. (1966), *Contributions from Schizophrenia to the Understanding of Normal Psychological Function,* Paper presented to the Eastern Psychological Association, 16 April 1966.

Shakow, D., and Juston, P. E. (1936), 'Studies of motor function in schizophrenia; 1. Speed of tapping', *Journal of General Psychology*, vol. 15, pp. 63–106.

Shannon, C. E. (1951), 'Prediction and entropy of printed English', *Bell System Technical Journal*, vol. 30, pp. 50–9.

Silverman, J. (1964a), 'Scanning control and cognitive filtering', *Journal of Consulting Psychology*, vol. 28, pp. 385–94.

Silverman, J. (1964b), 'The problem of attention in the research and theory of schizophrenia', *Psychological Review*, vol. 71, pp. 352–64.

Slater, E. O., and Beard, A. W. (1963), 'The schizophrenia-like psychoses of epilepsy', *British Journal of Psychiatry*, vol. 109, pp. 95–150.

Smythies, J. (1967), 'Recent advances in the biochemistry of schizophrenia', in A. Coppen and A. Walk (eds.), *Recent Developments in Schizophrenia*, Headley Bros., London.

Sokolov, Ye. N. (1960), 'Neuronal models and the orienting reflex', in M. A. Brazier (ed.), *The Central Nervous System and Behaviour*, Josiah Macey Jr Foundation, New York.

Sokolov, Ye. N. (1963), *Perception and the Conditioned Reflex*, Pergamon Press.

Sperling, G. (1960), 'The information available in brief visual presentation', *Psychological Monographs*, vol. 74, p. 29.

Spitz, H. H. (1963), 'Field theory in mental deficiency',

in N. A. Ellis (ed.), *Handbook of Mental Deficiency*, McGraw-Hill.

Spivack, G. (1963), 'Perceptual processes', in N. R. Ellis (ed.), *Handbook of Mental Deficiency*, McGraw-Hill.

Spivack, G., and Levine, N. (1957), 'The spiral after-effect and reversible figures as measures of brain damage and memory', *Journal of Personality*, vol. 25, pp. 267–77.

Spivack, G., and Levine, N. (1959), 'The spiral after-effect and measures of satiation in brain-injured and normal subjects', *Journal of Personality*, vol. 27, pp. 211–27.

Stennett, R. G. (1957), 'The relationship of alpha amplitude to the level of palmar conductance', *E.E.G. and Clinical Neurophysiology*, vol. 9, pp. 131–8.

Stepien, J., and Sierpinski, S. (1960), 'The effect of focal lesions of the brain upon auditory and visual recent memory in man', *Journal of Neurology, Neurosurgery and Psychiatry*, vol. 23, pp. 334–40.

Sternbach, R. A. (1960), 'Two independent indices of activation', *E.E.G. and Clinical Neurophysiology*, vol. 12, pp. 609–11.

Stevens, D. A., Boydstun, J. A., Dykman, R. A., Peters, J. E., and Sinton, D. W. (1967), 'Presumed minimal brain dysfunction in children', *American Medical Association, Archives of General Psychiatry*, vol. 16, no. 3, pp. 281–92.

Stott, D. H. (1960), 'Deliquency, maladjustment and unfavourable ecology', *British Journal of Psychology*, vol. 51, pp. 157–70.

Stott, D. H. (1962), 'Evidence for a congenital factor in maladjustment and delinquency', *American Journal of Psychiatry*, vol. 118, pp. 781–92.

Stott, D. H. (1965), *The Social Adjustment of Children*, Manual to the Bristol Social Adjustment Guides (third edition), London University Press.

Stretslova, N. L. (1955), 'The characteristics of some unconditioned reflexes in schizophrenics', *Proceedings of the All Union Theoretical-Practical Conference Dedicated to the Centenary of S. S. Korsakov and to Current Psychological Problems*, Med. Giz., Moscow.

Surwillo, W. W. (1961), 'Frequency of the alpha rhythm, reaction time and age', *Nature*, vol. 191, pp. 823–4.

Tait, A. C. (1968), 'The physiopathology of schizophrenia', in T. F. Roger, R. M. Mowbray and J. R. Roy (eds.), *Topics of Psychiatry*, Cassell.

Talland, G. A. (1963), 'Initiation of response and reaction time in ageing and with brain damage', in A. T. Welford and J. E. Birren (eds.), *Behaviour, Ageing and the Nervous System*, Charles C. Thomas, Illinois.

Tanner, W. P., Jr, and Swets, J. A. (1954), 'A decision-making theory of visual detection', *Psychological Review*, vol. 61, pp. 401–9.

Teuber, H. C. and Weinstein, S. (1956), 'Ability to discover hidden figures after cerebral lesions', *Archives of Neurology and Psychiatry*, vol. 76, pp. 369–79.

Thurstone, L. L. (1944), *A Factoral Study of Perception*, University of Chicago Press.

Tizard, B. (1962), 'The application of Luria's techniques to the study of normal schoolchildren', *Journal of Child Psychology and Psychiatry and Allied Disciplines*, vol. 3, pp. 175–84.

Tizard, J., and Venables, P. H. (1956), 'Reaction time responses by schizophrenics, mental defectives and normal adults', *American Journal of Psychiatry*, vol. 112, pp. 803–7.

Traugott, N. N., Balnov, P. H., Kauffman, D. A., and Luchko, A. E. O. (1958), 'On the dynamics of the destruction of orienting reflexes in certain psychotic syndromes', *The Orienting Reflex and Orienting Investigating Activity*, Moscow Academy of Pedagogical Science of R.S.F.S.R.

Venables, P. H. (1963), 'The relationship between the level of skin potential and fusion of paired light flashes in schizophrenic and normal subjects', *Journal of Psychiatric Research*, vol. 1, pp. 279–87.

Venables, P. H. (1966), 'The psychophysiological aspects of schizophrenia', *British Journal Of Medical Psychology*, vol. 39, pp. 289–99.

Venables, P. H. (1967), 'The relation of two-flash and two-click thresholds to withdrawal in paranoid and non-paranoid schizophrenics', *British Journal of Social and Clinical Psychology*, vol. 6, pp. 60–69.

Venables, P. H., and Wing, J. L. (1962), Level of arousal and the sub-classification of schizophrenia', *American Medical Association, Archives of General Psychiatry*, vol. 7, pp. 114–19.

Walch, R. (1958), 'Untersuchungen der Aufmerksamkeit mit einigen Testmethoden bei Hirnverletzten', *Psychological Abstracts*, vol. 32, pp. 72–90.

Ware, J. R., Barker, R. A., and Sipowicz, R. R. (1962), 'Performance of mental deficients on a simple vigilance task', *American Journal of Mental Deficiency*, vol. 66, pp. 647–50.

Weckowicz, T. E. (1957), 'Size constancy in schizophrenic patients', *Journal of Mental Science*, vol. 103, pp. 432–86.

Weckowicz, T. E. (1960), 'Perception of hidden figures by schizophrenic patients', *American Medical Association, Archives of General Psychiatry*, vol. 2, pp. 521–7.

Weckowicz, T. E., and Blewett, T. B. (1959), 'Size constancy and abstract thinking in schizophrenic patients', *Journal of Mental Science*, vol. 105, pp. 909–34.

Weckowicz, T. E., Sommer, R., and Hall, R. (1958), 'Distance constancy in schizophrenic patients', *Journal of Mental Science*, vol. 104, pp. 1174–82.

Weckowicz, T. E., and Whitney, G. (1960), 'The Muller-Lyer illusion in schizophrenic patients', *Journal of Mental Science*, vol. 106, pp. 1002–9.

Welford, A. T. (1958), *Ageing and Human Skill*, Oxford University Press.

Wells, C. E. (1962), 'Response of alpha waves to light in neurologic disease', *American Medical Association, Archives of Neurology*, vol. 6, pp. 478–91.

Wells, C. E. (1963), 'Alpha wave responsiveness to light and man', G. H. Glasser (ed.), *E.E.G. and Behaviour*, Basic Books.

Werner, H. (1946), 'Abnormal and subnormal rigidity', *Journal of Abnormal and Social Psychology*, vol. 41, pp. 15–24.

Werner, H. (1949), 'Disturbance with reference to figure-background impairment in brain-injured children', *Confinia Neurologica*, vol. 9, pp. 255–63.

Werner, H., and Bowers, M. (1941), 'Auditory-motor organisation in two clinical types of mentally deficient children', *Journal of Genetic Psychology*, vol. 59, pp. 85–99.

Werner, H., and Strauss, A. (1939), 'Types of visuo-motor activity in the relation to low and high performance ages', *Proceedings of the American Association of Mental Deficiency*, vol. 44, pp. 163–8.

Werner, H., and Strauss, A., (1941), 'Pathology of figure-background relation in a child', *Journal of Abnormal and Social Psychology*, vol. 36, pp. 236–48.

Werner, H., and Weir, A. (1956), 'The figure-ground syndrome in the brain-injured child', *International Record of Medicine and General Practice Clinics*, vol. 169, no. 6, pp. 362–7.

Williams, M. (1953), 'Psychophysiological responsiveness to psychological stress in early chronic schizophrenic reactions', *Psychosomatic Medicine*, vol. 15, pp. 456–61.

Williams, M. (1956), 'Studies of perception in senile dementia; cue-selection as a function of intelligence', *British Journal of Medical Psychology*, vol. 29, pp. 270–78.

Wilson, S., and Obrist, W. D. (1963), *Age Differences in E.E.G. Response to Different Stimulation*, Paper presented at American E.E.G. Soc., San Francisco.

Yacorzynsky, G. K., and Davis, L. (1945), 'An experimental study of functions of the frontal lobe in man', *Psychomatic Medicine*, vol. 7, pp. 97–108.

Yates, A. (1967), 'Psychological deficit', *Annual Review of Psychology*, Annual Review Inc., Palo Alto, California.

York, C. M. (1962), 'Behaviour efficiency in a visual monitoring task as a function of signal rate and observer age', *Perceptual and Motor Skills*, vol. 15, pp. 404–11.

Zahn, T. P., Rosenthal, D., and Lawlor, W. (1963), 'G.S.R. orienting reactions to visual and auditory stimuli in chronic schizophrenic and normal subjects', *Psychophysiological Newsletter*, vol. 9, pp. 43–51.

Zahn, T. P., Rosenthal, D., and Shakow, D. (1961), 'Reaction time in schizophrenic and normal subjects in relation to the sequence of a series of regular preparatory intervals', *Journal of Abnormal and Social Psychology*, vol. 61, pp. 161–8.

Zaslow, R. W., (1950), 'A new approach to the problems of conceptual thinking in schizophrenia', *Journal of Consulting Psychology*, vol. 14, pp. 335–9.

Zeaman, D. and House, B. J. (1963), 'The role of attention in retarded discrimination of learning', in N. R. Ellis (ed.), *Handbook of Mental Deficiency*, McGraw-Hill.

Index